DESPERATE RITES

Volume I:

ASTROLOGY AND THE OCCULT

IN THE

RICHARD SPECK MURDERS

By B.D. Salerno

I0122226

A sequel to *Richard Speck and the Eight Nurses: Deconstructing A Mass Murder* and a first in a series on the occult and metaphysical aspects of crimes.

Desperate Rites: Astrology and the Occult in the Richard Speck Murders

Desperate Rites, Volume 1

B D SALERNO

Published by B D SALERNO, 2023.

DESPERATE RITES: ASTROLOGY AND THE OCCULT IN THE RICHARD SPECK MURDERS

First edition. October 1, 2023.

Copyright © 2023 B D SALERNO.

ISBN: 979-8988478539

Written by B D SALERNO.

Also by B D SALERNO

Desperate Rites

Desperate Rites: Astrology and the Occult in the Richard Speck
Murders

Standalone

Richard Speck and the Eight Nurses: Deconstructing A Mass Murder
Richard Speck and the Eight Nurses: Deconstructing A Mass Murder
Anywhere But Here: Confessions of A Pisces Moon

Table of Contents

This work is dedicated to the memory of the eight nurses:

Pamela Lee Wilkening

Patricia Ann Matusek

Nina Jo Schmale

Valentina Pasion

Merlita Gargullo

Suzanne Farris

Mary Ann Jordan

Gloria Jean Davy

INTRODUCTION

It all began with an astrology horoscope. During the winter of 2020 I was seeking a new project for my astrology studies and decided to research the phenomenon of mass murder, a once-rare event that has now become an epidemic.

One mass murder had left its scar on my memory – the horrific Chicago massacre of eight student nurses in July 1966. I was a sensitive girl of fifteen at the time, and the brutal murders of these aspiring young women struck a painful chord in me. So naturally this heartbreaking crime headed the list.

But for reasons shortly to be explained, I had trouble trusting the actual time of the crime, which is required for any astrology horoscope. My uncertainty led me to yet more research, and as that research progressed, glaring inconsistencies and contradictions in the crime narrative began piling up. Before I knew it I was heavily engaged in investigating the murders, the likes of which I had never before attempted.

In May 2023 I published *Richard Speck and the Eight Nurses: Deconstructing A Mass Murder*. But my work wasn't done. As an astrologer I am familiar with some occult subjects – familiar enough to note them when they appear in crime stories, as they frequently do. My research yielded a plethora of references to coded numbers, pagan holidays, and occult ritual images, all of which suggested the involvement of a dark cult or organization – and this was before I had even analyzed the astrology of the case.

Once the physical door to the crime closed, a new metaphysical window opened, and I felt obliged to pass through it and revisit the crime with a view to exposing the occult themes embedded within. I alluded to the presence of a "hidden hand" in my book, and now here is an in-depth look at its ungloving.

Part I of the present book requires a basic familiarity with astrological terms and horoscope charts. Part II expounds on the occult themes and coded numbers that were sprinkled throughout the crime narrative, which went unnoticed in the aftermath of the crime - until now.

In his comprehensive book *A Dictionary of Symbols*, a vital reference for this work, mythologist and occult symbologist J.E. Cirlot tells us that "...crime is a feature of many desperate rites," many of which involve sacrifice. (p. 159) The act of crime itself is a desperate act, born of fear, anger, greed, or lust. Monumental crimes, such as the mass murder of the eight nurses, often display symbolic evidence of these desperate rites in the form of numbers, dates, persons, and imagery. Whether their appearance is random or deliberate, patterns of such appearances invite a closer look. I encourage the reader to learn these symbols and take that closer look. What you may see are the ethereal fingerprints left behind by the hidden hand.

PART I

ASTROLOGY

The Crime Chart

The Natal Chart of Richard Speck

The Eclipse Chart

The Natal Chart of Corazon Amurao

CHAPTER ONE
SYNOPSIS OF THE CRIME

At 11:00 PM an intruder broke into the back door of the two-story townhouse that served as a dormitory for eight nurses who were in training at South Chicago Community Hospital. Three were licensed nurses from the Philippines and the rest were American students who were to graduate just three weeks later.

The intruder went upstairs to the second floor where there were three bedrooms. He went to the room shared by Filipina nurses Corazon Amurao and Merlita Gargullo. Their door was locked. He knocked on the door. Corazon opened the door to find him pointing a gun at her. He commanded Corazon and Merlita to come out of the room and he also removed Nina (pronounced NIGH-na) Jo Schmale from the bedroom next door and marched the three of them down the hall to the largest bedroom, where three other women were already in bed.

He made them all sit on the floor in a circle, and then busied himself by cutting strips of cloth from a bedsheet on one of the beds. He tied their hands behind their backs and bound their feet together at the ankles with these cloth strips. During this time Gloria Davy returned home from a date and he tied her up as well. He then removed Pamela Lee Wilkening from the bedroom and walked her down the hall to Corazon's room where he fatally stabbed her.

As this occurred student nurses Suzanne Farris and Mary Ann Jordan returned from their evening out and he accosted them and forced them into the same bedroom where Pamela lay deceased. Mary Ann was also a nursing student but not a resident of the townhouse. Tragically, she had decided to spend the night at the townhouse with Suzanne, her best friend and future sister-in law.

The intruder viciously stabbed both Mary Ann and Suzanne. There was little commotion and no screaming during these horrific attacks. He then returned to the large bedroom and began taking one of the nurses out one at a time to the other bedroom where he stabbed and strangled Nina Jo Schmale, Patricia Ann Matusek, Valentina Pasion, and Merlita Gargullo.

Corazon Amurao had slid underneath a bunk bed during this time, where she remained hidden for a few hours. The intruder then sexually assaulted Gloria Davy on a bed near the bed where Corazon was hiding, then carried her downstairs to the living room couch where she was reportedly sodomized and strangled. The intruder returned upstairs to check the rooms but did not notice Corazon hiding under the bed. He left the premises at 3:30 AM.

At 5:00 and 5:30 AM the students' alarm clocks began to ring. Corazon, still underneath the bed, was able to shimmy out from under the bed and free herself from her bindings. She ran to her bedroom where three of her housemates lay deceased, and called out the window for help. Finally, she broke through the window screen to a second floor ledge where she shouted for help to passersby on the street below.

The next day Corazon identified Richard Speck as the killer and he was apprehended two days later in a flophouse in the Skid Row section of Chicago. He was convicted and initially sentenced to death, but the death penalty was repealed and he spent the next 25 years in prison. He died in 1991 one day before his 50th birthday.

Corazon gave statements to police that were contradictory, and her identification of the suspect initially caused confusion. She recalled the night of the crime in incredible detail down to the length of time the perpetrator spent with each victim, but at trial she could not recall vital details of the killer's appearance.

Her description of the events changed over time. Her account of the break-in was also suspect, as police found no means of forced entry, suggesting that a door was left unlocked or the killer was let in. Corazon had checked the front door but not the back door where the killer entered. Later on, events were added to the story that she had not recounted, and the crime scene and evidence were compromised many times over.

If the events of this horrendous story sound a little off to you, trust your instincts. Let's see what the crime chart has to say.

Regulus Platinum Professional 7 software was used in the creation of all charts.

CHAPTER TWO
THE CRIME CHART

Wednesday, July 13, 1966

11:00 PM, Chicago, Illinois, USA

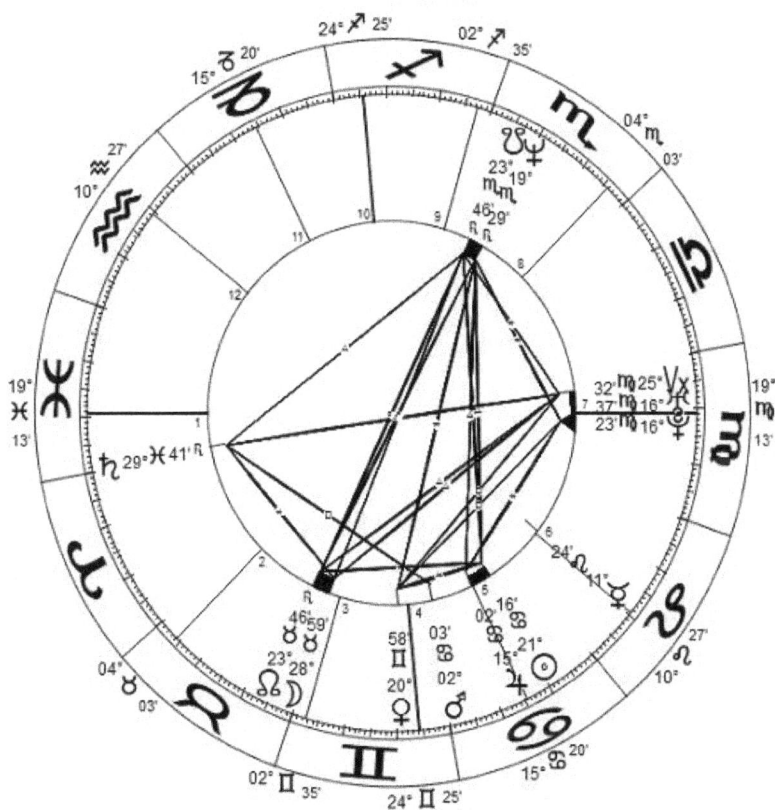

Pisces Rising

With 19 degrees of Pisces rising I expected to find a damaged and weakened Ascendant ruler, Jupiter. But here Jupiter is in its degree of exaltation at 15 Cancer. I had never seen such a well-dignified ruler for crime victims, let alone eight victims who had been brutally murdered.

Thanks to my tunnel vision I bypassed the fact that Jupiter was combust the Sun, and I wasn't using the outer planets as co-rulers back then, so nebulous Neptune also got lost in the shuffle. But the 11:00 PM time just didn't feel right, so I began searching for more confirmation of the hour, and the rest is history.

At that point everything changed. I became so absorbed in the crime research that I set the chart aside for the next three and a half years. Finally, with the physical review completed, I once again turned my attention to the metaphysical and occult aspects of the crime, which were substantial.

The mutable Pisces ASC suggests more than one victim, and there were eight victims. The same applies to the Descendant in Virgo. I think that there were at least two killers. Pisces rules hospitals and Virgo rules doctors and nurses. I believe that the motive behind the crime had nothing to do with Richard Speck and everything to do with the nurses' environment, which was the hospital, its doctors, and certain unethical practices that were taking place there. We'll look much more closely at that issue shortly, but now a retrograde, weighty Saturn at 29 degrees Pisces in the first house demands attention.

In a memorable lecture the late astrologer Buz Myers once described Saturn in Pisces as something akin to sin dipped in misery. Saturn in Pisces signals suffering and misery on many levels; it is the designation of the martyr who dies or is sacrificed for a cause. In this painful case

DESPERATE RITES: ASTROLOGY AND THE OCCULT IN THE RICHARD SPECK MURDERS

Saturn occupies the frenzied 29th degree of the last sign in the zodiac: desperate situations required desperate measures.

Retrograde Saturn, the master plan of the crime, was in a state of uncertainty and distress. I say this because Saturn rules the eleventh and twelfth houses of the chart, which concern friends, associates, colleagues, and large institutions like hospitals. Some participants in the murders may have had second thoughts, but a nefarious secret (Neptune in Scorpio in 8) had to be protected at all costs.

Neptune Overboard

Nebulous Neptune commands attention in the crime chart, telling us much of what we want to know, namely, that what we were told isn't necessarily true. In *Degrees of the Zodiac Symbolized,* Nineteenth Century astrologer Charubel doesn't hold back his disdain for the 19th degree of Scorpio, "the cursed degree of the cursed sign." (p. 30) It describes a person or situation that may become "a terror to society". His most chilling observation is the depiction of the degree as "a serpent with many heads, all in a circle...." According to the official narrative the nine nurses were made to sit on the floor in a circle while the intruder tied their feet and hands together, one at a time, before he took them from the room and killed them. The logo of serpents twisting around a staff, called the "caduceus," universally appears in medical illustrations. The symbolism of the degrees of the zodiac can be eerily literal.

As ruler of the ocean depths Neptune's influence runs silent and deep, with profound if unseen ramifications. Much of what it touches may never rise to the surface, and many things get swept away by its invisible undertow. Let's unpack the mysterious clues that Neptune guards in this chart.

Neptune is in the Venus degree of Scorpio, already conjuring images of a lustful secret affair and female reproduction. It rules saints and martyrs. The nurses were killed on the anniversary of the death of Saint Camillus de Lellis, patron saint of nurses and hospitals. Days later, five nurses were laid to rest on the feast day of Saint Camillus. There is a hospital named for Saint Camillus in Batangas, Philippines, the home province of sole survivor Corazon Amurao. This kind of eerie coincidence, or meaningful correspondence as I like to call it, appears frequently throughout this crime story, as we will see.

Richard Speck's favorite bar was housed in the Saint Elmo Hotel, so named after the patron saint of sailors (Neptune). Speck had just signed up for work as a seaman (Neptune) with the Coast Guard branch of the U.S. Navy (Neptune). He drank regularly and took drugs indiscriminately (Neptune) and on the night of the murders he was injected with a strange drug (Neptune) and lost all memory of that night.

First house and late-degree Saturn retrograde in Pisces brings out the worst side of Neptune: deception, fraud, trickery, and illusion. The ethereal tendrils of Neptune will entangle themselves well into Richard Speck's natal chart as well. Neptune is:

- Co-ruler of ASC, representing victims, five of whom were student nurses training in a local hospital, three were licensed nurses from the Philippines.
- In eighth house of murder, in Scorpio, sign of murder. Scorpio is the zodiac sign of the Philippines.
- Forms grand trine aspect with Sun, co-ruler of killers, and with partile trine to 19 degree ASC – water, water everywhere. The nurses' townhouse was a mile from the Calumet Harbor, the Coast Guard and Navy featured prominently in the story, the murder weapon (Mars, Cancer)

was dredged from the Calumet River (although it really
wasn't the murder weapon, and was excluded from the
evidence), Richard Speck was nicknamed "Fish Mouth," a
reference to Pisces, and a tip stated that he had been framed
in the crime as "bait," also referencing fish (Pisces).

- Scapegoat (Saturn) Speck was sacrificed (Pisces) to protect
  the real killers; he died at the age of 49 after spending 25
  years in prison for a crime he did not commit.
- Richard Speck drank alcohol and took drugs (Neptune) on
  the day of the murders and received an injection of an
  unknown substance (Neptune) prior to the murders, after
  which he suffered complete memory loss. Some have
  speculated that the drug was heroin, but Speck described that
  it came in a blue bottle (Neptune). Heroin normally comes in
  packets in powdered form, while drug preparations in blue
  bottles likely come from a pharmacy or a hospital (Neptune).
- Neptune/twelfth house references institutions and hospitals,
  and the twelfth rules secret enemies.
- There was an alleged suicide attempt (twelfth) by Richard
  Speck, which I believe was actually an accidental injury
  caused by broken glass (Moon in term of Mars).
- Richard Speck often stared off into space as if in a trance,
  with his mouth half open, which led to his nickname "Fish
  Mouth." (Pisces)
- A tip claimed that Speck was framed by a doctor who used
  him as "bait" - bait is used for fishing = fish = Pisces.

I have wondered whether drugs played another role in the murders.
Certain aspects of the crime scene indicate that no struggle took place.
While some of the nurses were reportedly bound at the wrists and
ankles this is understandable, but not all of them were tied up, leaving
room to wonder why they did not fight back. Evidence of bruising on
their necks suggested that someone had performed neck compressions

or chokeholds which may have rendered them unconscious prior to being stabbed or strangled. Or someone may have sedated them with a knockout drug, which would have been easily obtained from the hospital.

Drugs may fit yet another part of the scenario. Something amiss was definitely going on at the hospital, and this may have also involved smuggling. If some of the nurses had become aware of smuggling or drug dealing this too would have provided a motive for murder. Sadly, everyone in the house would have to die to eliminate any witnesses (sacrificed as collateral damage).

Neptune is prominent at every turn in the story. Speck frequented bars (Neptune), took drugs (Neptune), received a mystery shot (Neptune), lost his memory (Neptune), and hung out in bars with maritime names liken the Ebb Tide Tap, Kay's Pilot House, the Shipyard Inn, and stayed at the Saint Elmo hotel (patron saint of sailors). Sailors and saints will play other vital roles in the story as well.

Saturn the Timekeeper

Speaking of Neptune, Saturn tenants its sign and forms a tight trine to it within just minutes of arc. This treacherous duo are anathema to each other, yet are perfectly paired in the crime chart. Treachery, trickery, deceit, and cover-up were on the menu, and they were served up as masterfully as a command chef's performance.

As ruler of the eleventh and twelfth houses Saturn's first house presence also shows that friends, associates, colleagues, and the hospital were first and foremost in the victims' orb of activities. Saturn is in the Leo degree of Pisces, while Ascendant at 19 Pisces is in the Libra degree, which corresponds to my theory that a close friendship between hospital colleagues seeded the motive for these murders. Neptune also follows suit, being in the Libra degree of Scorpio. It calls to mind a jealous lover spurned and fear of exposure, which ended in multiple murder.

Pisces rising also conveys the mystical, the unknown, the unexplored, an aspect of our consciousness beyond the reach of our understanding. Pisces symbolizes fish – the arcane symbol of the "vesica piscis" is the shape of a fish, which in turn symbolizes Jesus Christ, who offered himself as the ultimate sacrifice to save humanity. Saturn in Pisces references sacrifice and suffering, much like what Christ endured in his final days. Catholics used to fish on Fridays to honor Christ, and some cultures serve fish for their Christmas Eve dinner. Fish swim in the nether regions of Neptune's domain, and were often the object of sacrificial rites in centuries past, just like their symbolic counterpart, Jesus Christ, who was often called "the fisher of men". There are ritual aspects to this crime, but these are for a later chapter on occult symbolism.

The first house of the victims is quite large, encompassing almost half the sign of Pisces and the entire sign of Aries up to early Taurus. Aries intercepted shows repressed anger and violence, which got its outlet in the killings. Mars in Cancer does not control its feelings well and is ruthless in its drive for self-preservation, often resorting to violence.

There's yet more to be said of Saturn. Seventeenth century English astrologer William Lilly, often called the father of horary astrology, stated that Saturn retrograde in the Ascendant destroys the question; "nothing goes well in the matter." While the crime chart is not a horary, one question is always in the minds of those who cast crime charts - "What really happened?" Lilly's proviso merits attention. And of course, nothing went well in the nurses' townhouse on that awful night of July 13, 1966. The question was not destroyed, but the lives of eight innocent young women were.

If anything, Saturn's ruining the question may be a signal that all was not as it seemed, and my study of the crime supports this. The public was fed a contrived narrative that misdirected the attention toward a shiftless loner, Richard Speck, and away from some real and threatening issues that had to be covered up at all costs, issues that involved hospital personnel and their illegal and immoral practices.

The first house lays the groundwork for the horror that was to transpire in the hours following. At the last desperate degree of Pisces and in its own term, there was no turning back for this malevolent Saturn, retrograde notwithstanding. Saturn in the final desperate degree and in its own term show cruelty and ruthlessness. The secret enemy ruler of twelfth was in the company of the nurses on the murder night.

The Moon and the Seven Weeping Sisters

Exalted but stressed Jupiter once again threw me a curve, this time because its dispositor, Moon, is also exalted in the sign of Taurus. The Moon co-rules the victims, who were all caring, nurturing women. The Moon sextiles the evil Saturn and is in the late degrees of Taurus. All late degrees are critical, as they fall under the term of malefic Mars or Saturn. Late degrees by necessity precipitate changes, sometimes borne of urgency or desperation.

Here the Moon is in the term of violent Mars and the Cancer degree. We also have Mars at 2 Cancer in the Taurus degree, which reinforces the theme: caring, nurturing women were subjected to anger and violence by stab wounds to the chest (Cancer) or neck (Taurus) or strangulation (Taurus, throat) and the murder plan was accomplished (2 is "best" degree of a sign, showing success). The Moon also occupies the same position as the fateful fixed star Alcyone, of the constellation Pleiades, and this offers us a glimpse into some very eerie occult connections to the story.

Also known as the Seven Weeping Sisters, the Pleiades represents seven sisters born to the mythical entity Atlas, whose daughters wept when he was condemned to carry the Earth on his shoulders. The star conveys violent influences, including death by blows, stabbing, and injuries to the face, including blindness.

Eight nurses were killed, but only seven were supposed to be present; the eighth, Mary Ann Jordan, had decided to spend the night with her best friend Suzanne Farris to discuss Suzanne's upcoming wedding to Mary Ann's brother Phil. Instead, the two were murdered side by side in one bedroom by several stab wounds (death by blows, stabbing), one of which struck Mary Ann in the left eye (blindness). And while this awful carnage was taking place no one reportedly screamed (a red flag during my research). While the Moon is normally well-placed in Taurus, its conjunction to tragic Alcyone, its sextile to the miserable Saturn, and its location in the term of violent Mars promised a tragic demise.

Venus

Next we move to Venus at 20 Gemini in the third house, the nurses' communications and attitudes. With Venus in the Scorpio degree there was probably some gossip or jealousy among the young women. Three of them were from the Philippines, and bonded through their common Tagalog language and culture, having been in the country only ten weeks. Four of the American students were close friends, while the youngest nurse, Pam Wilkening, friendly but shy, socialized more with friends outside the townhouse. The American and Filipina nurses were cordial, but not close. Aside from the common goal of a nursing career, the two groups shared little in common due to their disparate cultures and lifestyles.

Venus in Gemini suggests two-timing in a relationship, and squares the potent combo of Uranus and Pluto, close to the Descendant which represents the murderers. A volatile relationship brought about turbulent emotional clashes and threats of separation, even destruction, were afoot. The murders may have been the fulfillment of these threats. There's much more to be said of the unstable Uranus-Pluto conjunction emblematic of the Sixties.

Venus is in its own term at 20 Gemini, another possible connection to a relationship; so far we have ample references to Libra, Leo, Scorpio, and Venus, pointing to an intense affair or close relationship. Venus rules the intercepted seventh house Libra, and in the secretive Scorpio degree of 20, this knowledge was kept under wraps.

Venus conjoins the fixed star Capella. When afflicted, as Venus is to the Uranus-Pluto conjunction, Capella indicates jealousy and trouble, which is reinforced by Venus in Scorpio's degree. It's interesting that Capella means "little goat". The mythical story refers to a nurse, Amalthea, who raised the god Jupiter on goat's milk. A nurse who cared for baby Jupiter appears in a chart in which Jupiter rules the nurses – you can't make this stuff up. The fixed stars can be scarily accurate.

Capella may indicate a connection to the military, the Navy, or a religious affiliation. I believe all three were in play. I believe the killers had some paramilitary experience enabling them to kill quickly and efficiently. The Navy features prominently in the story because of Richard Speck's association with the Coast Guard and other persons who served in the Navy, and I use the term "religion" loosely, as significant references to Catholic saints kept turning up in my research, as well as powerful Catholic and Jesuit institutions like DePaul and Loyola Universities.

It's a little known fact that the police received a tip to the effect that one of the nurses was an "intimate friend" of one of the doctors at the hospital, and that the murders were wrongly blamed on Richard Speck.

DESPERATE RITES: ASTROLOGY AND THE OCCULT IN THE RICHARD SPECK MURDERS

I came to similar conclusions in my book on the case, in addition to other theories, and the stars support this possibility. But other nefarious things were going on behind the scenes too.

Fourth house Mars is in the Taurus degree of Cancer, where it lacks emotional control and discipline – violence in the nurses' lodgings. Mars represents men and rules first house intercepted Aries – an emotional man was in the background of this crime, and is disturbed about a woman (Mars in term of Venus). This man, or men, were present in the house on the night of the crime, and as Mars approaches Jupiter, they approached and overcame the student nurses and killed them. Mars and Jupiter in the fourth house place both victim and attacker in the townhouse that night.

Mars also rules the weapon and there were actually two weapons employed: a knife and strips of cloth which were cut from a bedsheet and used as ligatures to bind the victims and strangle some of them.

What was interesting in this case was that no knife was ever found or submitted into evidence. Police theorized that the convicted killer, Richard Speck, threw his knife into the Calumet River, and police divers searched that area of the river for the knife. On their final try they pulled up a pocket knife with a magnet (Mars rules metals and a metal device pulled up a metal knife). They assumed, but could not prove, that the knife belonged to Speck. The knife could not have been the actual weapon used because some of the knife wounds were much deeper than the knife's length. Mars in Cancer = weapon in the water. Bedclothes are the domain of Venus, so Mars in the degree of Taurus and term of Venus also designates the second weapon used – cloth strips.

Finally, Mars makes a 135-degree sesquiquadrate to Neptune, which I refer to as a "square and a half" – the knife was considered the murder weapon even though it did not qualify as evidence and it could not have caused some of the nurses' injuries. Deception and misdirection concerning the murder weapon are indicated by this aspect.

Rex Bills' *The Rulership Book* tells us that Venus rules eugenics. I believe the practice of eugenics, which was illegal in Illinois, was taking place in the OB/GYN rooms at the nurses' training hospital, and the trouble started from there. Doctors had performed tubal ligations on unsuspecting African-American women in at least two documented cases, and possibly many more. This is quite literally (and graphically) indicated by Venus (female) in Gemini (two Fallopian tubes) in square aspect to Uranus/Pluto (radical surgical intervention done surreptitiously without permission).

Now we arrive at the initial obstacle I faced when first tackling this chart: Jupiter rules the Pisces ASC, and so rules the victims. But how could beautifully placed Jupiter, in its degree of exaltation at 15 Cancer, possibly rule eight murder victims? I've since learned that 15 degrees is a degree of assassination, which is more appropriate to the case. My theory is that the murders were not the result of one lone gunman gone haywire, but a deliberate, targeted assassination complete with cover-up. This is borne out by the crime chart: The assassins knew the nurses, while Richard Speck did not.

Jupiter Beseiged

Jupiter is weakened by combustion with the Sun, co-ruler of the male perpetrator(s). Jupiter, showing the nurses, is caught between an angry, rash Mars and an emotional Sun in Cancer; there was no way out. The Sun is in the Sagittarius degree and I have wondered if one of the killers was a foreigner. There was a diverse staff of doctors from various countries at the nurses' training hospital. My research revealed connections between some of the doctors who were foreigners and some of the nurses.

DESPERATE RITES: ASTROLOGY AND THE OCCULT IN THE RICHARD SPECK MURDERS

The Sun trines deceptive Neptune; the killers covered their tracks well, and had some help with the cover-up. In fact, Sun, Neptune, and the ASC form a grand trine, facilitating the deception. Sun in the fifth further supports the belief that a love affair or attraction played some part in these murders. Here Jupiter was in range of combustion to the Sun, a literal depiction of the perpetrator doing away with the victims.

Jupiter is also in the Gemini degree of 15. Someone was going to blow the whistle on some activity in connection with the doctors at the hospital and this information was damaging enough and threatening enough to lead to murder. Venus in Gemini also presents this possibility.

With all the references to affairs, jealousy and out-of-control emotions, it is worth noting here that the chart establishes that the victims knew their killers. The killers also had knowledge of the layout of the townhouse. Richard Speck did not know the nurses, had never been to the townhouse, and had an ironclad alibi that everyone disregarded at his trial thanks to a skillful prosecution. The effect of misdirecting, sneaky Neptune was busy at work from behind the scenes; the prosecution spread a number of false narratives about the crime that my intensive research was fortunately able to debunk.

Bad Reception

Jupiter in Cancer, ruler of the nurses/victims, shows that they were living in a residence for higher education. Jupiter was also in the Gemini degree – the American nurses were students; the Filipino nurses were training in an American hospital. Jupiter was in the fourth house approaching the cusp of the fifth: six of them were at home (fourth house), three were out having fun (cusp of fifth). All but two were killed in two bedrooms.

Jupiter is exalted at 15 Cancer; however, the fifteenth degree is also associated with assassinations. Jupiter was within combustion range of the Sun, which co-rules the killers; the nurses were in mortal danger. Jupiter's dispositor is Moon, showing their maternal and comforting nature as nurses. However, Moon is conjunct the sorrowful fixed star Alcyone which describes Seven Weeping Sisters. There were eight victims because sadly, Mary Ann Jordan happened to be spending the night.

Saturn is in Jupiter and Neptune's sign Pisces in the Aquarius degree. A scapegoat individual, Richard Speck, was sacrificed to protect the real killers, and there are plentiful references to saints and holidays in this narrative, some of which have eerie connections elsewhere.

Relationships/associates are also strongly featured:

- ASC/DESC are in the Libra degree, as is Neptune
- Saturn is in the Leo degree
- Mercury, ruler of perps, is in the Aquarius degree

The chart is also overflowing with water signs and there is very little air; emotions and harsh feelings ruled the day. The murder weapon was thought to have been thrown into the Calumet River; the Calumet Harbor was within a mile of the townhouse; the presupposed killer had just joined the Coast Guard, and had been encouraged to do so by his brother-in-law, a former Navy man, who had also gifted him with a Navy-issue knife (not used in the murders); the killer was heard to run the water presumably to wash off his hands and knife.

Mars in 2 Cancer is a very informative placement. Two degrees, the degree of Taurus, is the "best" degree; the murder weapon was never found, although it could have been in the home (fourth). Six of the nurses were stabbed in the neck (Taurus), and chest (Cancer). Jupiter is trapped between Mars and the Sun; the nurses had no means of escape.

DESPERATE RITES: ASTROLOGY AND THE OCCULT IN THE RICHARD SPECK MURDERS

There had to be at least two killers to prevent any means of escape. It would have been difficult to pull this off if the killers were strangers, but as friends or associates known to the nurses (Aquarius), they could have easily staged a friendly visit and then, once inside, enacted their murderous plan. With such strong emphasis on Neptune I would not be surprised if the nurses were somehow surreptitiously drugged by means of a drink or an injection.

The medical examiner tested for barbiturates, which were detected in the case of one nurse who was taking phenobarbital, but no other types of drugs were included in the test.

Mars also indicates bruising, and bruises on some of the nurses show that they had been placed in some type of choke hold or neck compression that quickly rendered them unconscious and incapable of screaming or fighting back. Many have wondered why there was no screaming or resistance; but here the planets offer viable explanations.

The fifth house and the eighth house are inextricably linked to motivations for the crime. In my book I theorized that the murders were committed to prevent one or more nurses from getting the hospital in trouble. I had discovered through legal research that the hospital was engaged in illegal practices which some of the nurses may have found objectionable. That is not to exclude the possibility of an illicit affair between a nurse and a doctor, in fact, the two could have gone hand in hand – angry or jealous lover threatens to expose something illegal by the partner. It's complicated, as they say.

The fifth house rules children, procreation, birth control, pregnancy, and the eighth and Scorpio, surgery, abortions, and death. Legal research showed that certain doctors at the hospital had sterilized minority women without their knowledge or consent. The sterilization of an unsuspecting woman fits Neptune in Scorpio in the eighth, and the practice was done as a means of limiting the minority population (fifth = birth control). Saturn in the first house rules sterilization under subterfuge (Pisces). It places this important theme front and center in the chart.

Another note on Saturn, also referred to as "Father Time." The sole survivor remembered minute aspects of the night of horror down to how long the killer(s) spent with each victim – 20 minutes with one, 40 minutes with another, and so on. This was a remarkable feat considering that her hands were supposedly tied tightly behind her back for several hours, preventing her from seeing her wristwatch. But more than that, the official narrative demonstrated an obsession with time, pinpointing everything down to how many minutes each incident took. Time is Saturn's domain, and here an urgent final-degree Saturn called the moment-by-moment shots from the first house of the event right up to the event's final moments.

As Fate always has it, these moments were marked by the early morning ringing of the nurses' alarm clocks. Clocks = time = Saturn. Saturn, the eternal timekeeper and the Omega or end (as in death), holds a special place with the dark cults, who sometimes show an obsession with measurements of time. The Greek name for Saturn is Cronos, from which the term "chronology" derives.

Mercury Perpetrators

Now for a closer look at the perpetrators. Virgo on the Descendant rules both nurses and doctors. Ruler Mercury is in the sixth house of caretakers and healing helpers, although their role in this murder was anything but. Mercury is in the Aquarius degree of Leo, again emphasizing friends, colleagues, and love affairs. This aligns with the tip sent to police about one of the nurses being an "intimate friend" of one of the doctors. While the tip offered a possible motive for the murders it was at first ignored, then disregarded.

Mercury in Leo also signifies a person of distinction in his profession, someone held in high esteem, and the sixth house is the house of co-workers. This leaves little room for doubt that the perpetrators were medical staff associated with the hospital and therefore, were known to all the nurses.

What's the Point?

Let's break down the seventh house of the killers. The Vertex Point stands out in direct opposition to first house Saturn, and shows the literal point or purpose of the activity. 25 Virgo, in the Aries degree and term of Mars, shows angry doctors, and placed in the seventh house, a relationship with bitter feelings. This is yet another emphasis on the Libra/Leo/Venus/seventh house/fifth house affair gone wrong.

During the course of my research I came to the conclusion that Richard Speck most likely did not commit these murders and that the real perpetrators were connected to the hospital where the nurses were working or in training. It makes sense that those involved would want to misdirect attention away from themselves as much as possible. They had too much to lose – their licenses, their livelihoods, their good reputations. The point of the crime was to eliminate a worrisome relationship that proved too threatening a burden (Vertex opposite Saturn).

There were other concerns as well – illegal activities taking place inside the hospital operating rooms that could cause many problems for the hospital if word got out. During that sweltering summer of 1966 Chicago experienced an eruption of violent race riots whose flames would have been fanned by the exposure of illegal sterilizations of black women.

The Virgo Descendant is beset by its conjunction with the next destructive element in the chart – Uranus/Pluto at 16 Virgo. Like the Asc/Neptune tight trine, the conjunction of these two behemoths separates by only 14 minutes of arc. Uranus and Pluto together strafed the zodiac of the Sixties like the aircraft that carpet-bombed the Vietnamese landscape.

This cataclysmic conjunction was, fortunately, a once-in-a-lifetime event, as it will not be seen again until 2104. It fit the themes of the Sixties like a glove. Freedom-loving, willful, and often rebellious Uranus is not amenable with Pluto's heavy-handed, obsessive need and desire to control, manipulate or transform. Thus we had student demonstrations across the globe in protest of the Vietnam war, feminists burning their bras, civil rights demonstrations, and labor strikes, all of which resulted in violent clashes with law enforcement and the status quo.

The almost partile conjunction of Uranus and Pluto was highlighted the week of the nurses' murders: racial unrest culminating in riots, shootings and a partial shutdown of Chicago, anti-war protests storming college campuses, and most importantly, hundreds of nurses walking out on their jobs to demand better wages, treatment and working conditions. Revolution-minded Uranus in Virgo, the sign of health care workers, was fulfilling its potential, and when paired with Pluto, ignited a turbulence never before experienced.

Perhaps feeling empowered and encouraged by the women's rights movement, nurses in the mid-Sixties sought to reform and improve their profession by protesting low wages, poor treatment and unsatisfactory working conditions. During the same week as the murders 1,000 nurses had walked out on their jobs in California and more were expected to strike in New York and other areas. If Uranus in Virgo doesn't fit the definition of a labor strike I don't know what does. The nurses were waging economic war against a long tradition of being overworked and underpaid. Nurses' working conditions had been deplorable for centuries, but now women were standing up and voicing their concerns.

There was a dire shortage of nurses in the United States at the time. In 1964 President Lyndon B. Johnson signed the Nurse Training Act into legislation, which brought thousands of nurses from the Philippines to work in American hospitals. Thus Corazon Amurao, Merlita Gargullo and Valentina Pasion came to the U.S. to work at South Chicago Community Hospital. Although they already had their nursing degrees they also lived at the townhouse among the American student nurses.

It's interesting to note that Scorpio, so strongly highlighted by references to secrecy, cover-up, manipulation, reproduction, and surgery, is the zodiac sign for the Philippines. This is said only in the context of this story. I have known many wonderful Filipino individuals who do not match these negative qualities in the least, and some were both friends and doctors.

The mass murder of the nurses sent out a forceful subliminal message to women, especially those desirous of having their own career. In the years after the crime many nurses, haunted by the spectre of Richard Speck, feared being alone. One has to go out on one's own in order to become independent and pursue a career; the nurses were doing just that, and look what happened to them. They weren't living at home; they were on their own in a dormitory where a maniac broke in and massacred them. The same might happen to you – women desiring their own independence and career should be very afraid!

That's not all for Uranus/Pluto. It is close to the Descendant of the perpetrators and lends its characteristics to them: suppression of independence, like someone or something getting out of hand. Behind the desire to dominate and suppress lies a very deeply rooted fear, and here it was fear of exposure. The nurses' murders were motivated by the fear of exposure of certain things taking place at the hospital, and these are well described by Mercury in Leo: information about an affair. Leo also rules children, and the illicit practices at the hospital involved permanent birth control by illegal sterilization. This also connects to the eighth house Scorpio, a double reference to reproduction. The sterilizations were done under influence of Neptune (drugs, anesthesia, secrecy).

Neptune also fits in again to another part of the story. Richard Speck, the career criminal who was convicted of the murders, was a heavy drinker and took street drugs when he could get them. He also claimed that on the night of the murders two or three sailors (Neptune) invited him to get high with them. They injected an unknown drug (Neptune) into his arm and he was unable to remember the rest of that night (Neptune). He did not recognize the eight nurses from their photos (Neptune), and never recalled the events of that evening. If this isn't a hyper-Neptunian event I don't know what is.

The chart has explained that a cover-up was under way, that certain statements and persons were untrustworthy, and with Neptune's strong influence, things were not really as they seemed. If such is the case, can we trust the chart's information regarding the killers and their motives? Yes. By revealing the fraud the chart is merely the messenger; its integrity can't be breached.

Saturn is the planet rising. Among other things Saturn rules scapegoats – a scapegoat (Saturn) was sacrificed (Pisces) for the sake of the devious plot, as well as the unfortunate nurses. Saturn is approaching conjunction with Chiron at 26 Pisces (not shown in chart); the night would end with the tragic deaths of eight fatally wounded healers.

There is one more negative Piscean degree, and it is the 19 degree Pisces Ascendant, considered as "having afflictions during younger days" (p. 45) but things improve as time goes on. Sadly this was not so for the eight nurses, who did not live to see better times.

DESPERATE RITES: ASTROLOGY AND THE OCCULT IN THE RICHARD SPECK MURDERS

The Nodes of Fate

The Moon's South Node at 23 Scorpio is close to the deceptive eighth-house Neptune and to me that is the crux of the story – with Neptune as co-ruler of the nurses, we did not get the real story, and what was left behind – South Node, the evidence – was shaky at best, compromised and, in some cases, falsified. Twenty-three degrees of Scorpio is the Aquarius degree, again showing a connection to colleagues, associates, or a community.

Who were the Aquarian associates of the victims? I believe they were colleagues from the local training hospital, South Chicago Community Hospital, which served a low-income minority community. But there was another critical colleague, the only nurse who survived by hiding underneath a bunk bed – nurse Corazon Amurao. I have exhaustively examined her statements and trial testimony. When reviewed against the evidence and police reports I found them implausible and lacking in credibility, and I have discussed this at length in my previous book. Suffice it to say that the Aquarian reference to friends, colleagues and community takes on an even stronger meaning considering that a colleague and friend of the victims became the State's star witness. There was massive deception in the works.

A final note on Scorpio: one of the doctors whom I believe was involved with the murder plot was an OB/GYN specialist who was performing illegal sterilizations during routine gynecological procedures – can it get any more Scorpionic than that? This doctor was also a medical advisor to the Planned Parenthood Foundation and a staunch supporter of population control, a euphemism in those days for selective breeding, i.e., the elimination of non-white minorities.

We also have Mercury (killers) in Leo (children, birth control) in the sixth house of doctors, nurses, and co-workers. The crime chart

29

validates my theory that the murders were an inside job, courtesy of a corrupt hospital administration with a radical right-wing agenda. I believe a secret affair between a doctor and a nurse also lit the fuse for the murders with the threat of exposure of hospital secrets became a concern; the chart alludes to both possibilities.

Usually Mercury rules the witness, and here it also rules the perpetrators. I am not suggesting that Ms. Amurao committed the murders but I believe she had much more incriminating knowledge, and may have been threatened or coerced into telling a false narrative. In that regard, Ms. Amurao is also shown by the South Node – what was left behind was the sole survivor, but her story cannot be trusted (South Node conjunct Neptune in eighth house Scorpio). We still don't know the full story, although I hope my book sheds some new light on the horrific and senseless murders of eight lovely young women.

With the second house Moon and North Node (lies, deceit) in Taurus and the eighth house Neptune (insurance fraud), I have wondered whether the hospital held insurance policies on the nursing staff, including the eight nurses. While disturbing, this possibility is worth considering, especially in view of the Scorpio/Taurus/eighth house/money emphasis in the eclipse and crime charts.

A final curious note: Looking at the eighth house of death and murder we see South Node at 23 Scorpio and Neptune at 19. The murder address was 2319 E. 100th Street. This is yet another of the many eerie findings that inspired me to write this book.

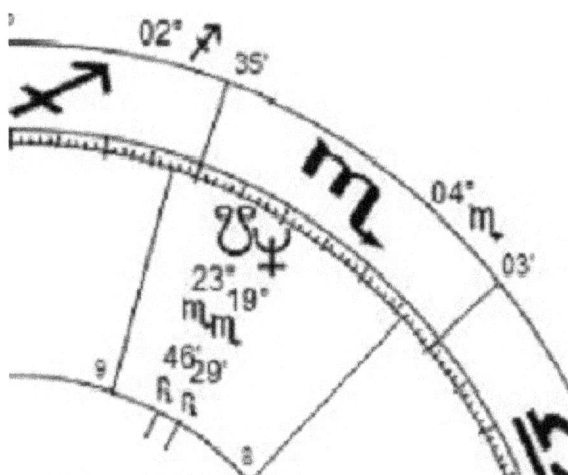

Prophecy of an Eclipse

Since ancient times solar (New Moon) and lunar (Full Moon) eclipses were considered the harbingers of future events, and this crime is one shining example. On May 20, 1966, there was a partial solar eclipse that lasted for over two hours, casting its influence two months into the future. The eclipse culminated with the Sun and Moon in a familiar degree: 28 Taurus, the same position as the crime chart Moon, with the same conjunction to Alcyone, the Seven Weeping Sisters of the constellation Pleiades.

The eclipse ruler is an unhappy Venus at 17 Aries, intercepted in the twelfth house, which is a huge house in this chart. She is an angry, petulant Venus with an ax to grind, and she is in mutual reception with first house Mars, which is also in its detriment in Taurus.

Venus is in the Taurus degree and disposits the planets in Taurus, showing an even stronger connection to the rising planets. The eclipse chart foreshadows the exposure of a secret, possibly romantic, in which several persons become embroiled, resulting in an extensive cover-up (Mars amid a stellium of bodies, with Mercury, in opposition to seventh-house Neptune).

The tight first house stellium in Taurus, clustered around the Moon's north node, is a compelling feature in the eclipse chart. Taurus suggests money, possessions, property, and their value. Mars rising in the Aquarius degree of Taurus describes civil unrest with property damage. Chicago's West Side neighborhoods were engulfed in chaos, rioting and gunfire during the week of the murders.

On the very day of the murders Illinois Governor Otto Kerner called in 1,500 National Guardsmen to restore order to the beleaguered city. Dozens of citizens and police were injured as a result of the rioting, seven policemen were killed, and over 200 citizens arrested. With the heavy emphasis on Taurus in this chart I wonder what became of those ruined, burned-out neighborhoods - whether they were bought on the cheap by investors for development or they reverted to their original state.

Whether it is an organic number or a deliberately coded number, 1500 is still an interesting number in this context. Centuries ago, the year 1500 was once thought to bring the end of the world, like an early prototype of Y2K. To residents of Chicago that July of 1966 it might have felt like things were leaning in that direction.

B D SALERNO

Solar Eclipse of May 20, 1966

4:44 AM, Chicago, Illinois

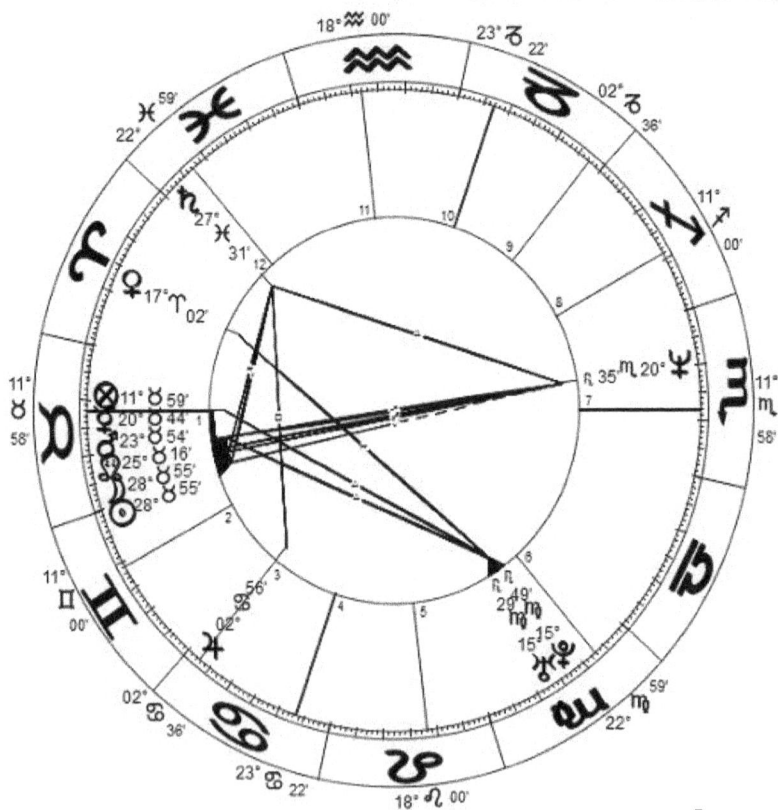

DESPERATE RITES: ASTROLOGY AND THE OCCULT IN THE RICHARD SPECK MURDERS

Neptune again exerts its shady influence, opposing the first house stellium, showing deceptive information and activities; no one will be clear on what is going on, as mayhem will rule the city of Chicago. Neptune opposes Mercury within just nine minutes of arc; major disinformation is about to spread concerning violence (Mercury/Mars conjunction opposite Neptune) and a subsequent cover-up. An angry Venus stalks the twelfth house of secrecy, self-undoing, and hospitals, just ahead of the miserable Saturn in Pisces promising pain and sacrifice.

CHAPTER THREE
NATAL CHART OF RICHARD SPECK

Richard Franklin Speck, a.k.a. Richard Franklin Lindbergh and Richard Benjamin Speck, was born at 1:00 AM on December 6, 1941 in the rural farming town of Kirkwood, Illinois. He was the seventh child in a family of eight, with several years' different between himself and his older siblings. At the last boy and the next-to-last child, he was spoiled and indulged by his mother, which was often a source of irritation to the rest of the family. All of them became respectable and hardworking citizens, except for Richard, whose main skill was the art of self-sabotage.

Speck was born on the eve of the Japanese attack on Pearl Harbor that launched the United States into World War II. Twenty-five years later he would bequeath a legacy of horror and destruction to the city of Chicago. It seems appropriate that the angles in his natal chart occupy the frantic, unpredictable last degree of the mutable signs. The child born on the precipice of a world war would become one of America's most hated mass murderers. The 29th degree of any sign is critical; it shows imminent change, sometimes chaotic, a turning point in a fateful direction. Like the hobby horses on a merry-go-round, Speck's life revolved around a series of crises, many of which he haplessly created for himself.

B D SALERNO

Richard Speck

December 6, 1941

Kirkwood, Illinois, USA

1:00 AM - Rodden AA Rated

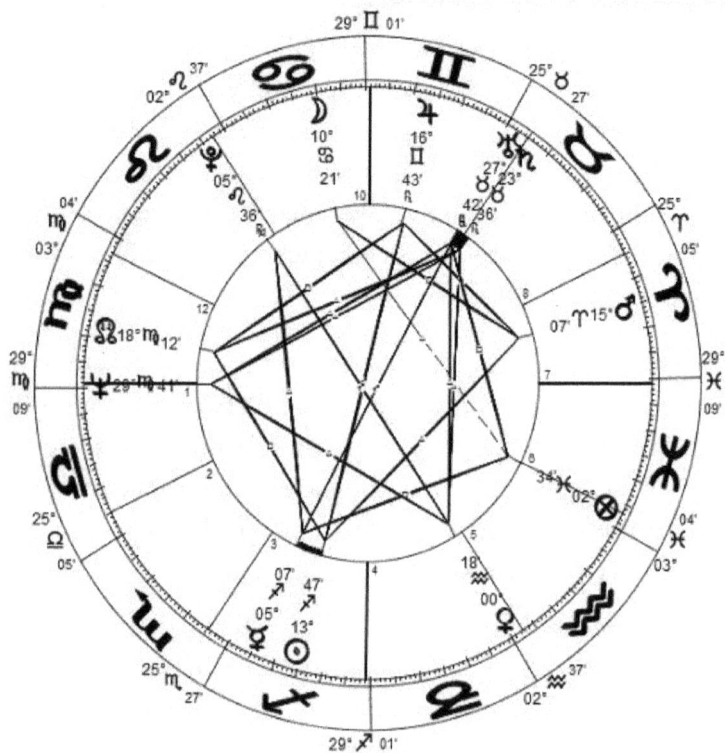

DESPERATE RITES: ASTROLOGY AND THE OCCULT IN THE RICHARD SPECK MURDERS

Even though 1:00 AM sounds like a rounded-off time, the Virgo ascendant suits Speck. He was tall (6'1") and lanky (160 pounds), with long arms and legs, and he was very particular about his personal grooming and appearance. He was neat and organized, fussy about his clothing, and always combed his longish sandy blond hair in the slicked-back "duck's tail" style popular in the 1950s.

His face was deeply pitted with acne scars (29 Virgo rising in term of Mars). Speck had a fair complexion, sandy blond hair and watery blue eyes that often stared off into space as if in a trance (Neptune rising). He was also addicted to drinking and enjoyed using various street drugs (Neptune), mostly pills with the colorful names "red birds" (downers), "yellow jackets" (uppers), and "goofballs," (self-explanatory).

Speck endured many severe head injuries (Mars in Aries square to Moon) while still a child, many of which were incurred when riding a bike (Mars in Gemini degree of Aries, afflicted Mercury in third). He was an accident-prone child (Uranus trine ASC, ruler of sixth Jupiter opposing Sun from third to ninth).

The ASC in his natal chart holds a powerful key to Speck's destiny: Neptune is rising at 29 degrees 41 minutes of arc in Virgo. Compare this to Saturn rising in Pisces in the crime chart: Both are exactly opposite each other to the exact degree and minute! This speaks volumes in terms of Speck's connection with the crime, as we will see. It also speaks of alcohol addiction, an enjoyment of street drugs, and a seeming addiction to theft and vandalism from his juvenile years into early adulthood.

Speck's early childhood was happy but short-lived. His father, Frank, died of a heart attack just after Christmas 1947. Speck had just turned six a few weeks earlier. His natal Saturn retrograde in the eighth house also reflects the early loss of the father, and transiting Saturn was making its first square aspect to its natal counterpart during this time.

The impact of father Frank's death left the large family in financial distress (Saturn in Taurus). Saturn pairs up with retrograde Uranus in Taurus and the two malefics straddle the ninth house cusp – Speck later became a juvenile delinquent (Uranus), turning to theft and burglary in response to the need for money and stability (Taurus) and breaking the law (ninth house).

His mother, Mary Margaret, chose for her second husband Carl Lindbergh, a traveling salesman. He was the opposite of genteel Frank Speck – an alcoholic with a bad temper and an intense resentment for spoiled young Richard. The stepfather is shown by Mercury, tenth house ruler, which is not only in its detriment but also combust the Sun and in partile trine to overbearing, oppressive Pluto. In 1950 Richard and his younger sister moved to Dallas, Texas to join his newly married mother, and it was all downhill from there.

Speck had his fair share of injuries, thanks to his abusive stepfather and his own reckless ways. He had suffered a number of concussions and serious blows to his head (Mars in Aries) while climbing trees or bike-riding (Mars in Gemini degree, Mars ruler of third). His impulsive and reckless behavior also resulted in many serious accidents (Aries Mars square Cancer Moon, Sagittarian Sun opposite Gemini Jupiter). After Speck's sudden death at the age of 49 an unusually high number of lesions and abnormalities were found in his brain (Mercury detriment in Sagittarius and combust Sun, Mercury oppose Jupiter in Gemini, Mars in the Gemini/Mercury degree sextile Jupiter in Gemini).

Richard devised a destructive plan to avenge stepfather Carl for his abusive conduct. He began to invade his stepfather's liquor cabinet, drinking whatever he could get his hands on. This habit persisted throughout his young adulthood, and he also added glue-sniffing and pill-popping to his adolescent resume. He took to running the streets with neighborhood gangs of older kids whom he yearned to impress, and together they would joyride, destroy property, drink in public and commit petit thefts (Mars ruler of third of neighborhood in Aries, in Gemini degree of youths, ASC ruler Mercury trine Pluto in eleventh of friends and associates).

The natal Moon reflects these early troubles: his Cancer Moon is in the Capricorn degree in the tenth house. Above all else he craved stability and security within the family, but it was not meant to be: Moon is in stressful square aspect to his seventh house Mars at 15 Aries, which speaks of domestic violence, between his parents and also directed toward him.

He carried this pattern throughout his early shotgun marriage to Shirley Malone, a fifteen-year old girl whom he met in October 1961, quickly impregnated, and married in January 1962. With the intercepted Moon he was barely aware of his own emotional needs, and his own internal conflicts expressed themselves in childish acting out and false bravado.

The Moon-Mars square also shows limited impulse control of his emotions and actions, and this lack of control led to most of his arrests for burglary, robbery, public intoxication, and disturbing the peace. With a Moon-Mars square the women in his life would be subjected to violence, and he was known to argue and fight with sex workers as well. As shown by the nature of the square from ten to seven, many of these disputes were in public places like bars or parking lots.

The Sagittarian Sun forms a trine to Mars; he was energetic, always restless and on the go, and possessed a strong sex drive. Mars is in the "assassin's degree" of 15 in violent Aries; he has long been considered one of America's most hated and feared mass murderers. The degree may connect an individual to a mass murder without his involvement, which I believe was the case with Speck.

He was often in the company of sex workers (Mercury from third trine eleventh-house Pluto). On the day of the crime he stole a gun from a sex worker's purse, (Moon square Mars) which was allegedly used in the crime, although the gun, improperly seized by police, lost, and then recovered, was disqualified as evidence.

The Sun trine the Gemini-degree Mars confirms Speck's agility with his hands, which were strong and supple. He was skilled at carpentry and manual labor and enjoyed his work as a deck hand aboard a freighter.

The feisty Mars is also in trine with Chiron at 14 degrees Leo in the twelfth house (not shown in the natal chart). Speck had extensive facial scarring from a severe case of adolescent acne, and the scars are unmistakable in all his photos. (Mars/Chiron = facial wounds or scars). His late Virgo ASC is also in the term or bounds of Mars, which rules scars and wounds.

Other distinctive feature were the numerous tattoos on his right and left shoulders and arms. These were publicized in the media and helped lead to his capture, even though the sole surviving witness testified that she did not see tattoos on the killer.

Mars in the Gemini degree of Aries references arm and shoulder tattoos.

Saturn in Taurus in the eighth reinforces a sense of scarcity and lack of resources. Coupled with the unfulfilled Cancer Moon Speck felt deprived of anything he needed on a physical or emotional level, which may explain why he resorted to stealing; most of his crimes were property crimes. Once he stole, he would drink up the proceeds, setting in motion the need for more money and the cycle of theft or bumming money off relatives. The eighth house Saturn trined his Neptune/

Ascendant, describing a pattern hell bent on continually feeding one's addictions.

He also drank to dull his incessant throbbing headaches, the result of brain trauma dating back to his accident-prone childhood (Sun in rambunctious Sagittarius opposite detrimented Jupiter in Gemini from third to ninth). He also suffered from poor memory, dizziness, and often faced what he called a "white blank wall" of visual and mental confusion when not engaging in alcohol or drugs.

Mercury rules the brain, and Speck's Mercury was in its detriment, Sagittarius, and combust the Sun in the third house. Speck had learning disabilities in school, and tested below average with an IQ of 87. Sagittarians tend to be immature, and this went hand in hand with his brash behavior. Detrimented Mercury in the third house is opposed by Jupiter; Speck was an attention-seeking braggart who would spin ridiculous tall tales of imaginary exploits. Fellow barflies were subjected to wild stories of drug running for a Mexican cartel and heroic combat in the jungles of Vietnam, neither of which were true. He craved the approval of his male peers, never feeling quite confident in his own masculinity or self-worth (Jupiter, ruler of Sun in detriment; Mercury, ruler of ASC in detriment and combust). His Sun-Mercury conjunction in the third house opposite the detrimented Jupiter in the ninth showed poor intellectual development, a tendency to boast, and a knack for getting in trouble with the law. These placements also reflect the poor judgment that got him in trouble on a routine basis.

With Uranus also occupying the ninth house, in trine to his ASC, Speck's frequent violations were his way of expressing his resistance to authority and rebelliousness. With Uranus in Taurus, he expressed it by committing property crimes - stealing valuables and money. He had the typical "juvenile delinquent" look of the 1950s, with his knife, leather jacket, and slicked back duck's tail. While still in Dallas Speck kept company with criminal types and ran with different gangs (Mercury in trine aspect to eleventh house Pluto).

Venus is in the zero degree of Aquarius, which is the pure expression of the sign. It is the mark of the non-conformist, but here opposes Pluto, so he broke from convention not as a visionary but as a career criminal. The opposition to Pluto also signals an extreme transformation of his sexual preferences. While in prison Speck either willingly or unknowingly took female hormones. He developed large breasts and with these new attributes became the preferred sexual "ride" of many inmates. This gender transformation has occult overtones and will be discussed later on. For now, Speck became the country's first transgender inmate, which shocked and horrified many at the time. But had they known how to read astrology charts, people would have understood the rationale: with natal Moon in a nurturing, feminine sign square aggressive Mars in masculine Aries, he was in conflict with his gender identity. His own psychiatrist noted his overreaction to homosexuals and theorized that Speck was harboring deep-seated homosexual feelings himself, which were given free expression in prison.

Mars trine wounded Chiron cues a lack of confidence in his masculinity, while Venus opposite Pluto brings pressure to bear on one's sexual orientation. With Pluto in the Leo degree, he was interested in as much sex, fun, and drugging as he could handle, and he enjoyed all of these while incarcerated in Stateville, one of the nation's harshest penitentiaries. It is no wonder that his heart finally gave out in 1991 just a day before his 50th birthday.

The North Node at 18 Virgo is in the twelfth house of secrets, secret enemies self-undoing, and large institutions. Eighteen degrees is considered an "evil" degree, but it doesn't necessarily mean that you are evil if one of your planets occupies it. It shows evil in the environment, or in the house in which it is placed. Richard Speck was a man of many demons, but there is another element at work. I believe he was set up to take the blame for the murder of the eight nurses; he had secret enemies behind the scenes (twelfth house), and was framed by doctors from the hospital where the nurses trained (Virgo, evil degree, twelfth house). This theory is elaborated at length in my previous book, *Richard Speck and the Eight Nurses: Deconstructing A Mass Murder.*

Speck and the Crime Chart

Fateful aspects crossed Speck's life map during the week of the murders and show an eerie destiny connecting him to the crime. Speck's Vertex point, 27 Virgo, opposes first house Saturn in Pisces in the crime chart. Recall that Saturn rules scapegoats. He was destined to be blamed for this crime, regardless of where he really was on the murder night. The Vertex point shows one's purpose; Speck's purpose was to provide a scapegoat for a heinous mass murder.

- The North Node in Taurus shows the alibi in the crime chart and Speck's Saturn conjoins it. Two tavern workers testified that he was in their establishment at the same time the crime was in progress. He was eating a hamburger. Taurus in Taurus' own house = food; North Node in Aquarius degree = community or associates. Speck socialized mainly with other barflies and bar employees; he was a loner who had no real friends. With Speck's Saturn in that same degree, the alibi, although an airtight one, was disregarded.
- The most telling feature of these aspects is that on the murder night, transiting Saturn was exactly opposite Speck's natal Neptune and his Virgo ASC to the exact degree and minute! Through official deception and much deceit, he was going to take the fall for the crime no matter what. From then on he would give the "appearance" (Ascendant) of being the mass murderer who killed eight student nurses. His Mars at 15 Aries is also in the degree of assassinations.

CHAPTER FOUR
NATAL CHART OF CORAZON AMURAO

Aside from the killers, Corazon Amurao, the sole survivor of the nurses' massacre, was also the lone source of information regarding the crime. All subsequent accounts of the crime were solely based on her recollection of the events of that evening, which I have called into question in my previous book. I believe that the crime narrative was a construct that Corazon was possibly threatened or coerced into promoting by powerful figures connected with the nurses' training hospital.

I do not have her exact time of birth, so I have cast the chart as a solar house chart. The Ascendant, house cusps, and Moon's position are unknown; the Moon was in either Scorpio or Sagittarius, depending on the birth time. While her natal chart is largely incomplete, a few aspects prove revealing.

Sun Opposite Neptune

Neptune, so prominent in the crime chart, also speaks volumes here. On the brighter side, the opposition indicates that she had many dreams and aspirations and that she was drawn to a higher calling in service to others. However, with the opposition aspect her view of reality was also challenged, and it rendered her susceptible to being drawn into illusion, fraud, and deception.

The opposition shows what we project outward, and as a result, what we draw in. Deception, trickery, and deceit usually follow swiftly on the heels of unrealistic goals and desires, and as an Aries she was likely to pursue her dreams with a me-first-only attitude. With Sun in the

Cancer degree of Aries she could be quite nurturing, but also fiercely self-protective.

Natal Chart of Corazon Amurao

March 26, 1943

Batangas, Philippines

Birth time unknown; solar house used

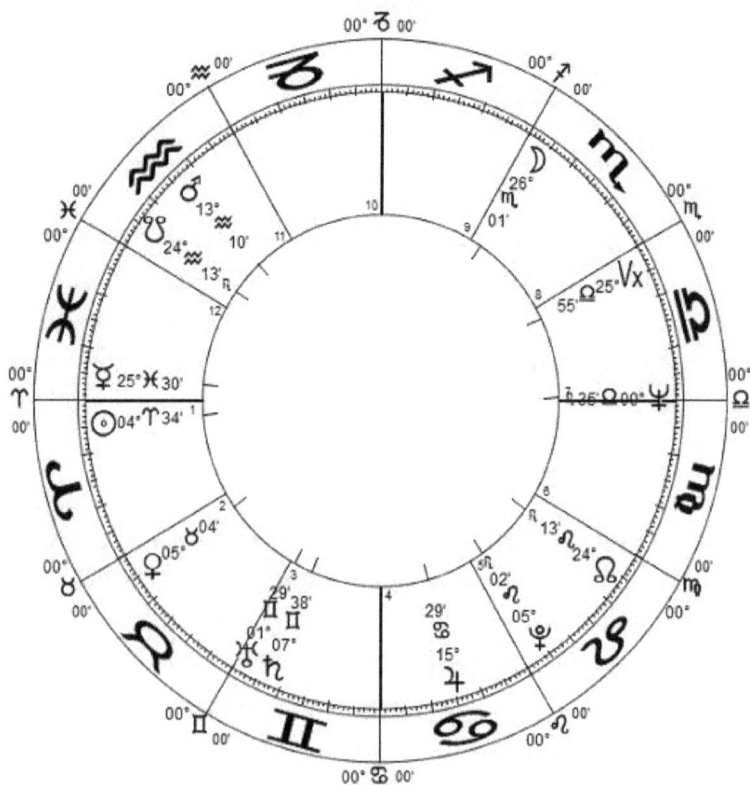

The Sun-Neptune opposition also indicates the possibility of falling victim to fraudulent schemes and activities, or being drawn into them by the influence of others. It conveys a talent for deception, and she was able to convince millions of people (still to this day) of the false narrative. I believe that the official crime narrative that she promoted was largely a construct created by those truly responsible for the mass murder of the nurses, and Corazon was used as their messenger.

Sun Trine Pluto

As sole survivor Corazon mesmerized the public with her bravery and her exceptional recollection of the night of the murders, and this is shown by the charismatic trine of Sun to Pluto. She was a petite, yet powerful, force to be reckoned with, and her testimony left no doubt that Richard Speck was the culprit who murdered her eight colleagues and housemates. However, both her testimony and identification were riddled with inconsistencies and contradictions that have escaped close scrutiny for well over 57 years.

The Sun-Pluto trine native is capable of great personal power and resourcefulness, but when under stress this power can be abused. There is a need to dominate and control, and the native instinctively understands how to fulfill this need, by manipulation, coercion, or other means. Sun-Pluto connections may also expose the native to criminal elements of society as well as the mass media and government officials (which may all fall into that same category). After the murders Corazon, now a celebrity, was wined and dined by government officials, and even invited Philippine President Ferdinand Marcos and his wife Imelda to her wedding.

In the immediate aftermath of the murders, and throughout the trial, Corazon maintained a calm, if not steely, demeanor in spite of the severe trauma of the ordeal. She never sought therapy or counseling.

This inner strength and reserve is also evident in her Sun-Pluto trine, which conveys a great capacity for self-regeneration and healing, as well as great self-control.

Venus square Pluto

Venus in Taurus is afflicted to Pluto, showing an aspect of intense jealousy and the need to meet one's needs regardless of the feelings of others. It shows a tendency toward obsessiveness in close relationships and a passionate nature that can enter "fatal attraction" territory if not kept in check. This aspect lends itself to volatile romantic relationships and the desire to get what one wants rather than what one needs. The desire for material security, money, and possessions, serves as a powerful motivator.

The Venus-Pluto square forewarns of difficulties in relationships, issues with abuse, stalkers, or associations with criminal elements, much like the Sun-Pluto trine. Mars in Aquarius widely forms a volatile T-square with Venus and Pluto, also introducing the possibility of violence, manipulation, or coercion, factors that I believe parlayed her into being an unwilling participant in a fraudulent narrative and subsequent cover-up.

The Silent Messenger

Corazon's Mercury at 25 Pisces is in a mute sign; she has never disclosed what really happened on the murder night and, now 80 years old, likely never will. The Piscean Mercury enjoys daydreams and fantasies, and with the force of her Plutonian drive she was able to achieve many of them: a comfortable life in the United States, a good job with a reputable hospital, and a sterling reputation in the true crime field.

Saturn's Touch

DESPERATE RITES: ASTROLOGY AND THE OCCULT IN THE RICHARD SPECK MURDERS

Saturn is in the Libra degree of Gemini; in an air sign, and associated with Libra, it presented Corazon with stressful challenges that she was able to turn to her benefit. Transiting Saturn was nearly exactly conjunct her Mercury on May 1, 1966, the day that she departed the Philippines for Chicago. This transition dramatically altered her life in ways that proved horrific at first, but ultimately beneficial. Transiting Saturn exactly crossed her Sun during the first week of April 1967 when she testified at trial and solidified her image as a brave, heroic survivor.

It's interesting to note that shady Neptune, so prominent in the crime chart, also makes it mark on Corazon, with the opposition to her Sun and co-rulership of Mercury. As for Mercury's other ruler, Jupiter made a return to its natal position during the week of the murders, and Corazon was fortunate enough to survive, even under suspicious circumstances.

With her Sun in sextile to both Uranus and Saturn she was uniquely disciplined to focus her will and her mind on something and achieve it. She displayed a tremendous ability to memorize a lengthy and challenging narrative in English, her second language, and convincingly win over the media, the courtroom and the jurors.

Based on these brief assessments Corazon Amurao was uniquely destined to fulfill her role in promoting the crime narrative. With her focus, determination, and sheer force of will she successfully navigated her way through a horrendous mass murder and escaped unscathed in more ways than one. I don't know the extent of her involvement in the murders, if any, or the extent to which she may have been coerced. In either case, though, two things are certain – she knows much more about the murders, and her survival instincts were stronger than anyone could have imagined.

PART II

OCCULT SYMBOLISM

CHAPTER FIVE
THE NUMBERS ADD UP

Numbers have great significance in occult symbolism. The importance of numbers is discussed in the Bible and many religious and philosophical tracts, and one practice that dates back many centuries is based on assigning numbers to letters. It is called Gematria. In this practice certain numbers have their own meaning and power, which are not known to the general public. Fortunately, more and more people are now learning about these coded symbols and applying the knowledge to understand that what is being shown to us is not the true, complete picture.

The prevalence of certain number patterns signals the workings of a hidden hand, acting as a warning that all is not really as it was portrayed. In my previous book I touched on the subject of the hidden hand behind the mass murder of the eight nurses. This hand reveals itself in symbols, like dates, anniversaries, and numbers. Some dark cults like to claim that they will always give a symbolic warning of some imminent planned evil before it happens so that we can be forewarned. But they know that the average person has no idea how to read their arcane coded language or their occult symbolism. I suppose this forewarning should be interpreted as an act of integrity – they followed through on their warning. But if a criminal tells you he's going to shoot you and then keeps his promise does that make him a man of integrity? Let's not forget that Lucifer's greatest talent is to cause chaos and confusion.

The numbers that feature prominently in the Speck crime narrative are 8, 11, 13, and 33. At times these numbers appear organically, but other times appear to have been inserted into the narrative to leave breadcrumbs for their hungry fellow cultists. (Hi there, it's Me, your friendly Hidden Hand!) In this crime story there were enough breadcrumbs to stuff a turkey. Let's unpack the numbers one by one.

Crazy Eights

While frequent, the occurrence of eights in the narrative is mostly organic, while the other numbers appear deliberately placed so as to signal their true origin. For example, Richard Speck was one of eight children - a fact, not a contrivance. However, he had an uncanny attraction to the number eight, which appeared significantly throughout his lifetime, and his story is consistent with the esoteric meaning of the number eight.

"All things are eight," states an old Greek proverb. (Westcott, p. 85) Saturn, aka Cronos or Omega, has eight moons; in Jewish mysticism eight events befall the damned, while the blessed receive eight rewards. The triple eight – 888 – is representative of Jesus Christ, the ultimate sacrifice for humanity. Eight when turned on its side represents infinity, the infinite cycle of suffering, death, rebirth, and resurrection. It is a lucky number to many Chinese because it also represents wealth. It is also known as the "beast" number.

Eight in numerology/gematria is a number of intense power, signifying death, transformation, and rebirth. These are the focal themes of dark cults; they are obsessed with amassing great power and wealth, and invest in death on a massive scale for the rest of humanity, which they believe is beneath them.

Eight corresponds to the zodiac sign Scorpio, which rules the eighth house of the horoscope. This house and sign are associated with the wealth (of others), death, surgery, transformation, sex as a reproductive act, the sex organs, insurance, taxes, and secrets behind the scenes. Scorpio's co-ruler, Pluto, was discovered in 1930, the same year that the atom bomb was under construction, and they go together perfectly. The number 8 can reference destruction on a massive scale. Eight and its energy appear often throughout the crime story:

- There were eight victims.
- Both Speck and Corazon Amurao came from a family of eight children.

- While imprisoned Richard Speck took female hormones to develop female breasts; this is very much an eighth house transformation involving sex. It is also an inversion, male-to-female, which is part and parcel of Satanic lore and practice.
- Speck participated in a garish video in which he performed oral sex on a prison partner and flaunted his breasts for all to see. The video was made in 1988. It was a mockery of the prison system, and possibly, the entire Speck case.
- Speck's older sister Shirley, born October 26, 1922 (26 reduces to 8), died on October 26, 2020 at the age of 88.
- The doubling of a number increases its power. Richard Speck was sentenced to death by electrocution on June 5, 1967, with the execution scheduled for September 1, 1967 – exactly 88 days later, double death. However, the death sentence was commuted to 400 to 1200 years in prison, with a range of 800 years between them = 8. Naturally, he would die centuries before the sentence would be fulfilled, but it's interesting how the 8 fits the time span.
- Speck's childhood address was 908 W. Boston Street. 908 reduces to 17, then down to 8, and this address will reappear in a later discussion.

- He allegedly killed 8 nurses, leaving one survivor. 1 + 8 is discussed below.
- The prosecution of Speck, the sacrificial fall guy, rested on the

eighth day of the trial and in its eighth week of presentation. It is interesting that the local newspapers saw fit to call these repeating eights to their readers' attention.

- Aces and eights. The combination of 1 with 8 or 18, derived from Jewish tradition, refers to "Chai," meaning "life," but it also has other meanings. There are 18 blessings in the Hebrew liturgy. The legendary Wild Bill Hickok was allegedly holding two pair, aces and eights, in his poker hand when he was shot and killed. Aces and eights are a coded message indicating that there's something off with the official story. Eight nurses were murdered; one survived, and my research has shown that something was definitely off with the story.
- There was one trial for eight murders, 1 / 8.
- Eight is also the single reduction of the number 17 – 1 + 7. Seventeen also confers great power over one's enemies and is considered a number of victory.
- Corazon Amurao claimed that not one of the women screamed during their horrible ordeal; all she heard were several gasps of "Ah!" Why "Ah?" This may be a reach, but A-H is the combination of the first and eighth letter of the alphabet = 1 + 8. Aces and eights again, and again, something's off with this account. A and H are also the initials of Nazi leader Adolf Hitler, and some of the authorities were engaged in the practice of eugenics. 1 + 8 in this code does not reference "life". The initials of one doctor, John Harrod, who was performing illegal procedures on black women in the nurses' training hospital, had initials J or 1, and H, or 8, again 1 + 8, but he was hardly a pro-lifer.
- The Knights Templar, thought to be forerunners of the Masons and many subsequent societies, formed their first order in the year 1118 CE – aces and eights, and the year

totals to 11, the next power number in the story.

Eleven, the Ascending Portal

The number 11 is very significant in this crime story. It brackets the action: The intruder knocked on the door at 11:00 PM; Speck awoke the next morning at 11:00 AM. The 11:00 PM time is suspect; Corazon also told police that the intruder knocked at midnight, but while questionable, 11:00 PM has always been given as the correct hour. This 11 may be a breadcrumb inserted into the story for those "in the know". As for the 11:00 AM time, Richard Speck claimed that he awoke "around 11:00 AM," and was seen by a witness at his hotel shortly thereafter, so this time is probably accurate.

Eleven is considered an unbalanced number; it is one more than ten, a number of completion, and one less than twelve, which symbolizes divine order. In medieval Europe eleven was called "the devil's dozen," (p. 241 Biedermann) and corresponds to "the focal point of symbolic inversion and antithesis," (p. 234 Cirlot), signifying a negative situation or outcome. Think 9/11, or 11/22/1963, the date of the JFK assassination, the original Veterans Day, 11/11/1919, or the address of the Idaho murders of four college students, 1122 Kings Road, committed on 11/13/22.

Even the occultists are wary of number 11. "Eleven is the essence of all that is sinful, harmful, and imperfect ... destruction, violence, defeat, and death," and it is also "the number of sins." (p. 100 Westcott)

There is a physical dimension to the number 11. The silhouette of the Twin Towers, or World Trade Center destroyed on 9/11/01, resembled a number 11 reaching up to the skies. "Twins" suggest a 1 plus a 1, like the zodiac sign Gemini. Two columns or pillars pointing upward symbolize man's reaching toward the heavens to become God-like. And who are capable of planning and building such structures? Architects and builders, who centuries ago founded the society of Freemasonry. Freemasons refer to God as the architect of the universe, even including the letter G in their logo. The two pillars of Solomon's Temple play a significant role in their history. "There is a divine influence and connection between objects and their physical placement and measurements" (Cirlot, p. 62)

Now we need to review the July 29, 1966 cover of *Life* magazine (29 reduces to 11 and 7 + 2 + 9 = 18, aces and eights).

LIFE magazine did a comprehensive piece on the murder of the nurses. The magazine cover is the most bizarre-looking cover photo that I have ever seen. I had to look at it for a full minute to get my bearings as to what it was about. Occult symbolism can do that to you.

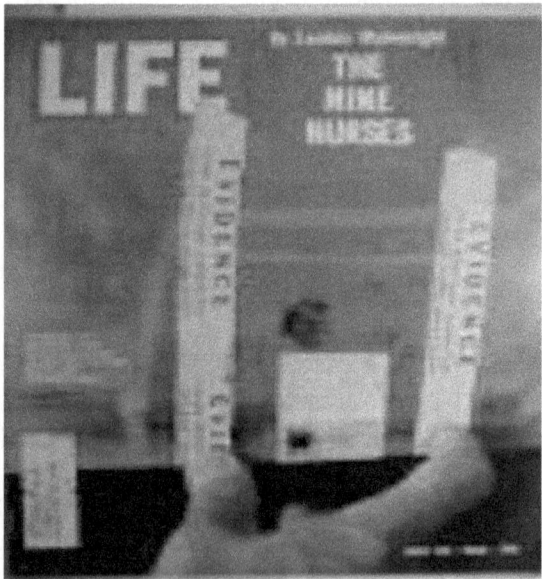

The photo shows a portion of the door to the south bedroom that had been sectioned off by white strips of police tape marked EVIDENCE to show where one of three fingerprints of Richard Speck was found. At bottom of the cover a man's thumb and index finger bracket the two strips of white EVIDENCE tape below the smudged print.

At first I didn't understand what I was looking at until I realized that this was a section of the inner door to the south bedroom – the bedroom into which the nurses had been herded prior to being tied up. Three latent partial fingerprints of Richard Speck were supposedly lifted from this door, which had been turned on its side in the photograph - but why? The fingers are not pointing to the fingerprint, or to the posted white note; they are showing us a symbol – the two tapes which clearly form the number '11.'

The door didn't have to be shown sideways; the posted note could have been placed upright next to the fingerprint, with the EVIDENCE tapes facing sideways. But then we wouldn't have seen what was intended: the representation of the 11, a coded signal that a plan was afoot and all was not as it seemed. And all these signals were given in plain sight, but only for those "in the know". Can anything be more "in plain sight" than the cover of the country's most popular magazine?

A clandestine group had left its calling card on the south bedroom door and on the cover of a magazine with tens of millions of readers. The two tapes, resembling pillars, with the square piece of paper between them, evoke the shape of a temple; Solomon's Temple was an extremely important building in the lore of the Knights Templar and subsequent Freemasonry.

This image had a deeper meaning: 11, the number of those who strive to be God-like. We had already endured the misery of 11/22/63, which was a double-11 event, but were still 35 years away from that other "11" date that would live in infamy: September 11, 2001. Eerily, and scarily, the *LIFE* magazine cover featuring "The Nine Nurses" plus the 11 symbol references 9-11.

The tower is a determinative sign denoting height or *the act of rising above the common level in life or society*. Basically then, the tower is symbolic of ascent." (p. 344 Cirlot)

What is implicit in these observations that only certain people are capable of "rising above the common level," by creating such structures. The tower symbolizes a class of people who consider themselves above the rest, and whose acts, intended to be understood by only a select few, are justifiable. They may create the rules, but the rules don't apply to them. These symbols of numbers and images suggest that an organized group orchestrated and carried out the murders following in their agenda. I have proposed a few theories relating to nefarious activities connected to the hospital, which some dark cults have been known to support.

On the subject of rising above the common level, was Richard Speck, an itinerant seaman with a penchant for drinking and drugs, a long rap sheet of burglaries, thefts and other violations, a below-average IQ of 87, and a limited education, capable of constructing a sinister scenario of this depth and sophistication? Or was his role created for him in advance, without his knowledge or even his participation?

As noted, Speck entered the townhouse at 11:00 PM and awoke at 11:00 AM the next morning. Sole survivor Corazon Amurao told a police commander that the intruder entered at midnight, but this record never made it into the story, and the time remained at 11:00 PM. I believe this eleven was inserted into the story to leave a breadcrumb. Like terrorists, secret cults or groups believe in announcing their intentions, albeit symbolically. I believe this eleven was critically placed into the story for just this purpose. After all, why couldn't he have shown up at 11:30 or spookier yet, midnight? That eleven had to get into the picture. And that wasn't all.

The eleven makes other appearances in this crime story:

- Speck had eleven defense witnesses at his trial – eight family members, and three others. Two of them, a bartender and his wife, provided an ironclad alibi – that while the murders were in progress Richard Speck was sitting in their tavern eating a hamburger.

- Referring to the astrology in Part I, Mercury, denoting the killers in the crime chart, is at 11 degrees Leo. Leo indicates that they held positions of authority, and you also have the evil 11.

- The alleged robbery began on the night of July 13. 7 + 1 + 3 = 11. This date is also important for other reasons to be considered shortly. Let's now look at history's favorite unlucky number – the ever popular thirteen.

Thirteen, a Twin and Cousin Prime

Thirteen is considered both a lucky and an unlucky number. Lucky for those who like to gamble, but unlucky for enough people that building developers deliberately leave out the thirteenth floor in hotels and multi-level residences. In mathematics 13 is a "twin prime," being only two numbers from 11, and is a "cousin prime" at a distance of four numbers from the powerhouse 17. As the fifth, sixth, and seventh prime numbers, 11, 13, and 17 are a potent lineup. This crime story is fraught with symbolic numerical references that point far away from the shiftless lone gunman Richard Speck and strongly toward an influential group of power brokers who had strong associations with the hospital and even stronger connections to an ideology that favored selective breeding of the few and the eradication of the many.

Thirteen relates to the original unlucky Friday the Thirteenth in the year 1307 when followers of the Knights Templar were imprisoned, tortured and executed. The date of July 13 was the last and the worst day in the lives of the eight slain nurses and I believe it was chosen for a few reasons.

- It was the eve of the anniversary of the death of Saint Camillus de Lellis, patron saint of nurses and hospitals. Dates are very important in ritualistic activities. As things turned out, most of the nurses were buried on July 18, the Feast Day of Saint Camillus. The eighteen is 1 + 8, aces and eights. This crime was not the work of a bumbling burglar by any stretch of the imagination.
- What is the significance of the dates July 13 and 14? I have two ideas about that.

1314 AD is the year in which Jacques de Molay, spiritual leader of the Knights Templar, was executed after an imprisonment of seven years. Were both dates intended to convey the message that the murders were the workings of a clandestine group descended from the Templars? The second idea is that pagan holidays are celebrated on their eve, and carried over into the next day, so that the murders had to begin on the eve of Saint Camillus' death day and end on the anniversary day.

- 713 adds up to 11. In gematria, when "seven hundred thirteen" is spelled out using a reduction cypher, it results in 103. In numerology the zero is disregarded, so that 103 becomes 13. The 7-13 date fit the bill in more ways than one.
- 713, when flipped upside down, spells "lie" - L – 1 – 3.
- There were 41 witnesses for the prosecution, 41 being the 13th prime number.
- The date 7/13/66, or 7 + 1 + 3 + 6 + 6, equals 23, symbolic number of an ancient cabal of power brokers. Note that the

address 2319 E. 100th Street contained this number 23, the ninth prime number, while 19 is the 8th prime number. We have discussed eight, and nine is also significant, as it represents an ending, or 3 + 3 + 3, or 3 x 3. Three's form the basis of nine.

- Outside the U.S. the 7-13 date is shown as 3-17, which is also significant, as numbers are reversed or inverted in occult practice. March 17th is another Catholic holiday, Saint Patrick's Day. Interestingly, 317 is the 66th prime number, and if transposed to 137, you get the 33rd prime number, a major breadcrumb for ritual events.

A brief note on 23: It refers to to a powerful cabal invested in dominating world events. In the Nineteenth Century occultist W. Wynn Westcott described this group as the 23 Councils of the World. Note that the chosen time of the crime, 11:00 PM, is also the 23rd hour in military time. Twenty-three also connects to 8 as it is the eighth prime number.

The second portion of the address, 19, contains the number 1, which represents the beginning, and 9, which represents the end.

The Inevitable Number 33

It was reported that 33 fingerprints were found at the crime scene. This number is significant to the society of Freemasons. The highest level a mason can obtain is the 33rd degree. Many of our politicians, Presidents, legislators, judges, military, and celebrities were high-ranking Freemasons or belonged to related groups which are too numerous to mention.

Thirty-three also has Biblical and spiritual significance. Jesus Christ lived to be 33 years old; King David of the Jews ruled for 33 years.

Numbers obtain their power by being added together three times, so that 33 is actually the sum of 11 + 11 + 11. Adding together the numbers of the date July 13, 1966 yields 33: 7 + 1+ 3 + 1 + 9 + 6 + 6 = 33. Going back to 17 for a moment, 17 + 17 + 17 = 51, another power number. Think Area 51 or May 1, (5/1), which was not only May Day in Europe but the founding date in Bavaria of Adam Weishaupt's influential group of Illuminati, May 1, 1776. Outside the U.S. this date would be shown as 1-5 and as we've already seen in Part I, 15 degrees in Astrology relates to assassination.

It's not surprising that the Illuminati were founded by Adam Weishaupt in Ingolstadt, Germany, which was, appropriately, the home town of the fictional character Frankenstein. Weishaupt was a professor at the University of Ingolstadt in Bavaria where Mary Wollstonecraft Shelley, author of *Frankenstein*, was a student. She published her book in 1818 – a year of aces and eights!

Here is another look at 3 11's: when added, 11 + 11 + 11 = 33 but when cubed, 11 x 11 x 11 = 1331 = 13 and 31, a palindrome. When reversed, numbers retain their same power, as we have seen with 51 and 15, but palindromes introduce the effect of mirroring, which is very powerful in occult ritual practice. In a nutshell, mirroring invites another dimension or reality into the process, which is one purpose of a ritual – to effect a change on a situation, thereby introducing a different outcome or reality.

Some final notes on the 33 include a look at the reverse ordinal cypher used in gematria. Many keywords in this crime narrative – fall guy, scapegoat, false flag, and US Navy, all reduce to 33.

DESPERATE RITES: ASTROLOGY AND THE OCCULT IN THE RICHARD SPECK MURDERS

The official crime narrative tells us that the murder night began at 11:00 PM and ended at 3:30 AM. I used Corazon Amurao's extremely detailed account of the events of that awful night to construct a timeline. Following her own precisely given estimates, it would have ended well after 4:00 AM, but regardless of the timeline the architects of the crime narrative always stuck to 3:30, which minus the colon and zero = 33.

Another notable number was 22, the combining of 11 + 11. This number appears organically in the story, and that may be all it's worth, except that it has a curious connection to dark history.

According to the official narrative, Richard Speck stole a gun from a sex worker on the afternoon of the murders and he used this gun to threaten the nurses during the robbery. Corazon Amurao could not identify the gun, which was later improperly seized by police and therefore inadmissible as evidence. In fact, the prosecution continually referred to the gun a pistol with live cartridges in its clip when the gun was actually a revolver, which has a rotating cylinder and not a clip.

The revolver was a Röhm .22 calibre purchased from a mail order retailer of firearms. Oddly enough, Röhm was also the name of a highly ranking Nazi official, Ernst Röhm, who headed Hitler's SA security force until Hitler saw fit to assassinate its members and replace them with the much feared SS. We have doctors practicing eugenics at the nurses' hospital, occult ritualistic themes, and significant dates sprinkled throughout the narrative. Even numbers that seemed to appear organically, like .22, and the name of a prominent Nazi officer, fit the bill, whether intended or not.

We end up with a predominance of the numbers 8, 11, 13, and 33 in the Richard Speck murder case, all of which have significance to dark cults. We have the spectre of eugenics, or the purification of the white race, a Nazi ideology, in play. Now we should consider the imagery of the crime and the messages it broadcast to a fearful and horrified public.

CHAPTER SIX
OCCULT IMAGERY

Ritual Aspects

There were many ritualistic aspects of the mass murder of the eight nurses besides the numbers. In the official narrative presented to us, the following events stand out:

- The intruder knocked four times on the door to the northeast bedroom. As mentioned, three knocks on a door is part of a Freemason ritual initiation.
- The intruder had the women sit in a circle with him in the center. What cults *don't* perform rituals in a circle?
- He then cut up a sheet and tied them up one by one, their hands behind their backs and their feet together at the ankles.
- He then removed the ankle ligatures before taking each woman from the room, one at a time, first to the northeast bedroom where he killed three, then to the northwest room where he killed three by means of stabbing and strangulation. One was left across the bathroom threshold, and one on the first floor living room sofa. No bodies faced East.
- The women were reportedly passive and went without a struggle, evoking the image of silent permissive maidens being calmly led to sacrifice. It was a horrifying image that I, an impressionable young girl, couldn't erase from my mind for weeks afterward.
- Between killings he took care to wash his hands and knife, as in a purification ceremony. Water formed part of the ritual; even the Calumet River got into the act.

As the story went, Richard Speck walked 1.6 miles to reach the nurses' townhouse, during which time he had to cross over the Calumet River on his way there and back. Water and bodies of water play an important role in occult murders; the police even dredged a penknife from the river and attributed it to Speck, although the knife could not have made several of the victims' wounds. We have already noted the mention of water in Part I regarding Neptune.

- "Calumet" is a derivation of colonial French, and refers to a pipe fashioned from reeds and used in peace ceremonies by Native Americans. The name of the river references a ritual ceremony.

- The violation of the feminine was also at work here. Stories circulated that the nurses had been raped, tortured, and molested, which was not true. Corazon Amurao even gave a detailed description of the rape of Gloria Davy, which took place on a bed near the bed where she was hiding. Police also claimed that Gloria had been viciously sodomized, although the pathology reports noted that her genitalia appeared normal and "unremarkable." The sexual desecration of the female body had to make its way into the story, even though the medical examiner himself refused to confirm that any such violation had taken place.
- First was last. Corazon initially told police that Gloria Davy was the first woman to be killed (at which time she did not mention the rape at all). She then changed her statement to claim that Gloria Davy was the last to be killed. Vital facts were reversed.

Red, White, and Dark

DESPERATE RITES: ASTROLOGY AND THE OCCULT IN THE
RICHARD SPECK MURDERS

Images and colors penetrate the substrata of our unconscious minds far more deeply than we are often aware, and much in the same way crimes register a damaging effect on the collective psyche. The mass murder of the eight nurses dealt a severe blow to the public on an emotional and psychological level. Although I lived comfortably far from Chicago - 800 miles (another 8) - the headlines EIGHT STUDENT NURSES SLAIN still delivered an emotional gut punch. To add emotional insult to psychic injury early news broadcasts delivered a volley of gruesome information that wasn't even true, as if the murders themselves weren't horrible enough.

The crime narrative featured three significant colors. We were told that the intruder was dressed in all black. It is common garb for the burglar who strikes by night, but it also touches us on a more primal level. Black, the absence of color and light, is by nature ominous or evil. Black represents the dark, where bad things happen unseen, and many are afraid of the dark. Black is the color of Saturn and Scorpio, the bad guys so prominent in the crime horoscope.

By contrast, the traditional dress of the nurse is all white: white caps, dresses, stockings, and shoes. From head to toe the professional nurse wears white, the combination of all colors and the symbol of purity and innocence. It's not surprising that the checkerboard featured in Freemasonry has alternating black and white squares.

The third and final color was red; the crime scene was very bloody. Blood is both the essence of life and the symbol of death. This crime gave us the colors black, white, and red, which appear in the garb and rituals of Satanic and other dark cults. The gruesome carnage offered the ultimate union of opposites – white (light-life) and black (dark-death), synergized by pools of red blood.

Gloria's Nightmare

The crime also featured another dark-cult principle: the devastation and destruction of all things feminine and nurturing. The feminine, creative spirit is not revered by the dark cults. In this regard a curious story circulated regarding Gloria Davy, who was supposedly the last nurse to be taken from the room and murdered.

Corazon had managed to slip underneath a bunk bed near where Gloria was lying. Unbelievably, Corazon recounted that Gloria had fallen asleep on one of the bunk beds while her roommates were being led out of the room, one by one, to their deaths. When the killer finally came for Gloria, the last victim, he startled her from a deep sleep. She blurted out, "I dreamed my mother died!" (This report did not appear in Corazon's first version, in which Gloria was the first to be led from the room and killed).

The idea that someone under threat from a knife and a gun, tightly trussed up with ligatures and held captive by a stranger who has just robbed her, could simply doze off while her friends and roommates were disappearing at knifepoint from the room one by one, is preposterous. Whoever constructed this part of the narrative was brazen enough to add a dash of bizarre symbolism.

"I dreamed my mother died," injected an eerie sense of foreshadowing, as Gloria was facing her own fragile mortality. Or perhaps the story of the dream allowed for a bit of occult symbolism, which is rife in the official narrative, and in my opinion, intentional.

The death of the mother has deep psychological ramifications. It is the death of the maternal, feminine spirit, all that is nurturing and comforting, which is embodied in the image of a nurse-caregiver. The loss of such a supportive person in one's life is emotionally devastating, as those who have lost their mothers, especially in in tragic ways, can attest. Someone behind the curtain was having too much deranged fun planting paranormal woowoo that Gloria foresaw her own death. The grieving public had to be reminded that nurses are like our mothers, penetrating our already wounded psyches on an even deeper level.

The reference to death of the mother always eerily foreshadowed what I believe was one motive for the murders: certain doctors were performing illegal tubal ligations on black women at South Chicago Community Hospital, a secret that could not afford exposure. The doctors were robbing their female minority patients of any chance at motherhood. "I dreamed my mother died" may have served as a sadistic jab at what really lay behind the killings.

Something About Gloria

Some eerie correspondences in the circumstances surrounding Gloria's death dragged me down a fascinating rabbit hole. On the night of the murders she heard her favorite song on the radio, "You'll Never Walk Alone," as her fiancé was dropping her off at the townhouse after their date. She remained in the car to hear the entire song, then bid her fiancé goodnight and entered the townhouse for the last time. She then telephoned her mother, as she did after every outing, and told her, "I'm home now, Mom. I'm safe."

"You'll Never Walk Alone" was a big hit from the 1945 musical "Carousel," by Rodgers and Hammerstein. The immensely popular musical was later made into a movie in 1956. I was very familiar with both songs. The vinyl LP soundtrack to "Carousel" shared space in my record rack with LPs by Gerry and the Pacemakers.

In the story of "Carousel" the main character, Julie Jordan, mourns the death of her husband, Billy Bigelow, who fell on his knife and died of a stab wound during a botched robbery attempt – shades of what would befall Gloria and her fellow nurses. The lead character, Julie Jordan, shares the same last name as Mary Ann Jordan, the unfortunate student nurse who was spending that night as a guest.

Death by stabbing during a robbery gone amok. The tragic story of "You'll Never Walk Alone," Gloria's favorite song, served as an eerie testament to her final moments.

And that wasn't Gloria's only connection to the music of the times. In December 1965 a rock band called The Shadows of Knight released a hit single, "Gloria," ("G-L-O-R-I-A") which rose to number one in the band's home city, which happened to be, of all places, Chicago. The song was a hit throughout 1966. In a sinister, almost otherworldly reference to the events that transpired in the shadows of Gloria's last night, The Shadow of Knight's recording company was Dunwich Records 666.

Rat Lines?

Corazon's heroic image provided excellent optics for the Philippines, which had recently formed an alliance with the United States and begun sending humanitarian aid to South Vietnam. This legislation was enacted right around the same time that the Philippines began sending trained nurses to fill vacancies in American hospitals.

With all due respect to all the wonderful Philippine nurses who came here and served the patients in our hospitals, the opening of borders from Vietnam through the Philippines and on to the United States also provided opportunities for less humanitarian acts, such as trafficking – in arms, drugs, contraband, or people. The discovery, and threat of exposure, of that type of activity would certainly have provided ample motive for a mass murder, even of innocent students nurses.

Also noteworthy is the fact that the Philippines was also sending "psywar" agents to conduct psychological operations in Vietnam – shades of Project Phoenix, a creation of Lieutenant Colonel Michael Aquino, a psyops specialist and original member of Anton LaVey's Church of Satan, founded on an important pagan date, April 30, 1966.

DESPERATE RITES: ASTROLOGY AND THE OCCULT IN THE RICHARD SPECK MURDERS

This was one month after the founding in London of The Process Church of the Final Judgement which has been implicated in the Sharon Tate mass murder. A lot of suspicious scary cults were sprouting that infamous spring of '66, and the perpetrators of the nurses mass murder may have been members.

More Subliminals

Another intensely disturbing image invoked by the crime is one that might have come from a bad 1950s zombie movie in which eight young maidens are passively led to their deaths like sacrificial lambs. This subliminal message discouraged passive resistance and favored fighting and violence and relates to one story that circulated widely after the murders.

It was said that the nurses remained passive throughout their ordeal because of their training, and that Corazon Amurao had tried to convince her housemates to resist, but no one did. As a result, all were killed except Corazon, the only one who wanted to fight back. In the context of the Vietnam war that was raging at the time, and the strong anti-war movement, this message resounded, don't be passive, fight! Eight nurses were passive, and look what happened to them.

The suggestion of passivity, so strongly inserted into the official narrative, implied that they went willingly, as if in a trance. This image alone is a form of collective hypnosis; by being told that no one screamed or resisted, we were forced to wonder what really happened and how it could have happened, and thus relive the crime over and over again in our own minds. We were entranced and entrapped by its brutal imagery.

Years later, as a true crime fanatic, I recalled that sick gut feeling every time I read about Richard Speck and the eight innocent nurses. I am grateful to have stumbled upon the opportunity to study the crime and debunk the lies that were told to us. I only hope that others with better skills and more resources will also take an in-depth look at this crime and discover more revealing information.

The Crux of the Matter

A media report of a mass murder will likely conjure up mental images of random bodies strewn across a landscape saturated with blood and mayhem. However, the nurses' crime scene appeared well organized and even staged to convey symbolic messages:

- The first murder, of 20 year-old Pamela Lee Wilkening, reportedly occurred in a bedroom that occupied the northeast corner of the house. In Masonic practice the cornerstone of a building is always set in the northeast corner of the building plot. Was this coincidence, or by design?
- This northeast bedroom was reportedly where Richard Speck, who had already broken into the house, had knocked four times at the door, which was opened by Corazon Amurao, the sole survivor of the massacre. Why a burglar would force entry into a home and then knock on an interior door beggars belief, but I wondered whether this was a. Three knocks on a door is part of a Masonic ritual initiation. Although there were four knocks here, I still had to question it, as the notion of a burglar knocking on a door seemed ridiculous – especially since he first had to walk past two open rooms with women's pocketbooks in plain sight.
- Pamela Wilkening, Suzanne Farris, and Mary Ann Jordan were also slain in the northeast bedroom. The three of them lay side by side on the floor, with their heads facing north. From left to right, Mary Ann was face up, Suzanne was face down, and Pam was face up. The three bodies were bloody but neatly arranged side by side.

- Patricia Ann Matusek was murdered just outside the bathroom, face up, with her head facing west. On the first floor living room sofa, Gloria Jean Davy was lying face down, her head facing south. No one's head pointed toward the East. East represents the dawn, the rising of the morning sun. I wonder if the failure to face the East was deliberately intended to symbolize the ending of the nurses and of the situation that had motivated their deaths.

- Three women were then murdered in the northwest bedroom: Nina Jo Schmale, Merlita Gargullo and Valentina Pasion. Nina Jo was lying face up on her bed, with her head facing west. Nearby on the floor were Merlita Gargullo and Valentina Pasion, their bodies lying in a shape resembling an 'x.' I originally theorized that Valentina's killer became enraged after she scratched him, leaving particles of his skin under her fingernails and a scratch on his face. In his anger he then forcefully threw her body across Merlita's. But they were both lying stretched out, with arms down, as if deliberately placed in the 'x' form. What could this possibly mean?

CHAPTER SEVEN
THE SAINTS GO MARCHING IN

'X' Marks the Spot

In occult symbology the 'x' is known as the "crux decussata" or the cross of Saint Andrew. Andrew was the brother of the apostle Peter; it was Andrew who introduced Peter to Jesus Christ. When Andrew was persecuted for his Christian beliefs he was sentenced to be crucified on the cross, but he objected; he was not worthy to be put to death like Jesus, and demanded that the cross be changed from a 'T' shape to the shape of an 'X'. That shape became forever identified as the cross of Saint Andrew the martyr. The crime chart highlighted the sacrificial aspect of this crime and the very strong Neptune alluded to the presence of saints and sacrifice.

Saint Andrew's Order of the Scottish Rite of Freemasonry have their own chapter in Chicago. They even have a Facebook page! Was this 'x' placement of the bodies of Valentina and Merlita another breadcrumb?

J.E. Cirlot, a Spanish poet, mythologist and symbologist, describes the cross of Saint Andrew as "a symbol for agony, struggle and martyrdom." (p. 69) The Piscean/Neptunian reference to saints and martyrdom has been discussed at length in Part I Astrology.

Regarding the 'x' Cirlot also relates that the 'x' is a symbol of inversion, and also refers to symbolic numbers:

"The numerical expression of Inversion seems to be two and eleven. Symbols of inversion are: the double-spiral, the hourglass, the drum shaped like an hourglass, St. Andrew's cross, the letter X ... and, in general, all that is X-shaped." (p. 159) The 'X' is two lines crossed, signaling inversion. (I have wondered why the mercurial Elon Musk found it necessary to change the name of Twitter to X, but this gives me some idea.)

The principle of inversion is important in the practice of dark cults. Inversion relates to the reversal of opposites: White/Black, Death/Life, Up/Down, In/Out, Female/Male, and so on. Satanists/Luciferians, many of whom are Hollywood celebrities, have had their children undergo sex changes to honor their beliefs in homage to the Fallen Angel.

Getting back to two, it is a number of balance, polarity, and opposites, and can also be shown as two one's, as in II, or 11. Thus, two becomes eleven, and vice versa, signaling the inversion described above by Cirlot. Crossing these two lines results in the 'x' – they are inseparably bound together.

Forensic Messages

The pattern of the nurses' wounds was also revealing. No single killing was like the next, and certain areas of the bodies appeared to be the main targets. One nurse was stabbed in her left eye, a possible dark cult reference; one was stabbed in the heart, and one had her throat slashed – was this a message that they had seen too much, cared too much, or talked too much about something that needed to be kept quiet? These patterns are also suggestive of Mafia-type assassinations, and I have theorized that professional killers participated in the mass murder.

A final note on the placement of bodies: There were three bodies in the northeast bedroom, three in the northwest, one in the hallway, and one on the first floor. 3 + 3 + 1 + 1, which can be seen as 33 and 11, or, 13 and another 13. Three has great significance in the Bible, as it references the Holy Trinity, and it is also a preferred number in Freemasonry symbolizing perfection and divinity. There are three stages of Freemasonry; 3 and 3 become 33, the highest degree attainable, and we have already noted the power of 33. The placement of the eight bodies gives us another 33 and another 11.

We now have as occult figureheads the presence of Saints Camillus and Andrew, but there's more. Another saint that fits eerily into this strange mosaic is Saint Elmo, the patron saint of sailors.

Elmo/Erasmus the Martyr

Like his saintly colleague Andrew, Elmo, (or Erasmus of Formia), died as a martyr who was persecuted and tortured for promoting Christianity in the Roman Empire. In his honor Fort St. Elmo was built as a protective fortress in Valletta, on the Mediterranean isle of Malta, as well as St. Elmo Bridge (think Knights of Malta, a powerful clandestine society to which George H.W. Bush belonged, as well as the singer/actor Sammy Davis, Jr.) There is also a Saint Elmo fortress on a hill in Naples, Italy. Interestingly, Elmo/Erasmus of Formia was martyred in the year 303, or, 33.

Two silent films were made about Saint Elmo, both issuing in 1923, which oddly is the murder address, 2319, transposed.

I traveled down this rabbit hole when I first learned that Richard Speck was in Chicago to find work as a merchant seaman, and that he had stayed for a time at a flophouse in Chicago known as the Saint Elmo Hotel. The Saint Elmo housed his favorite bar, Pete's Tap House, a frequent setting in this story. Note that Saint Andrew introduced his brother Peter, who later became a saint, to Jesus, and here we have a Pete referenced along with Saint Elmo!

Saint Elmo is a fairly common name for establishments catering to sailors, and a few iconic restaurants in the Midwest bear the name. As previously noted, saints play a role in the rites of clandestine groups. Saint Elmo was the name of a secret club of Yale University, like the better known Skull and Bones, Scroll and Key, Berzelius, or Book and

Snake. The Saint Elmo, however, has the lowest ranking by wealth of Yale's secret societies, which may explain why it is nowhere near as well known as Skull and Bones, which boasts past members George H.W. Bush, George W. Bush, John Kerry, and William Howard Taft, to name a few.

Like numbers, symbols and not-so-coincidental events that populate this research, one historical detail tops it all off. In 1894 the Saint Elmo Hotel in Fort Worth, Texas, which bore the name of alleged mass murderer Richard Speck's favorite lodging, was bought by the notorious Dr. H.H. Holmes, known as America's first serial killer. Holmes, who committed a fair share of his murders in a Chicago hotel, had in mind to refurbish the place, but a visit to the hangman in 1896 permanently interrupted those plans. Speck and Holmes shared the Dallas-Chicago connection, along with Jack Ruby.

Here is a triple of eight's: Dr. Holmes' initials, H-H-H = 8 – 8 – 8. Henry Howard Holmes was a big departure from his real name, Herman Webster Mudgett, and had a much classier ring to it. Holmes was a phony doctor and a con man who claimed between 20 and 200 murder victims. What was this strange man *really* involved in?

True crime is stranger than fiction. Speck had worked as a 7 Up delivery truck driver in Dallas, and one establishment along his route was the Carousel Club, owned by the notorious Jack Ruby. Speck liked to tell the story of when he cheated Ruby out of $36 by shorting a beverage delivery of a few cases. The murderer of a Presidential assassin was cheated out of money by a man considered one of America's worst mass murderers. You can't make this stuff up.

It seems the deeper you dive beneath the surface the more intricate and surprising are the snarled webs of evil deeds. Here we have numbers, sailors, saints, a doctor, hotels, murders, murderers, and a few cases of 7Up.

DESPERATE RITES: ASTROLOGY AND THE OCCULT IN THE
RICHARD SPECK MURDERS

Yale's Saint Elmo society was initiated in 1889 as one of a consortium of eight of the university's secret societies. After a long period of inactivity it was revived in 1965 and opened for membership. In November 1966 (11/66), eight male and eight female students were to be inducted into the society. To those in secret clubs of this nature the numbers really matter: 8 – 11 – 66 (which is twice the power of 33).

An induction ritual involving eight young female students took place four months after the ritualistic murders of eight young student nurses in a city where the alleged murderer frequented a hotel named after its namesake saint – coincidence, or meaningful correspondence?

Saint Walpurga's Night

One more saint appears on the periphery of this crime story, and she is Saint Walpurga, an Anglo Saxon Catholic missionary and martyr who was canonized into sainthood on May 1, 870 CE by Pope Adrian II. Note the 51 from May 1, which is the sum of 17 added three times.

May 1 is the May Day holiday in Eastern Europe as well as the birth date of Adam Weishaupt's Illuminati club. Unlike Saint Camillus, Walpurga was put to death for her support of Catholicism, but like Camillus, her death anniversary is celebrated. Walpurga's night, or *Walpurgisnacht*, is celebrated on April 30, a sacred day in the pagan calendar much revered by the Third Reich.

Richard Speck's trial began in Peoria, Illinois, on April 3, 1967, and concluded on April 30, 1967, *Walpurgisnacht*; it started on 4-3 and ended on 4-3 (or written as 3-4 if outside the U.S.) The zero in 30 is dropped, so that 4-3 holds the same power as 4-30. Anton LaVey's Church of Satan was established in San Francisco on April 30, 1966. Naturally that date was pre-selected for its pagan significance. Adolf Hitler supposedly committed suicide on April 30, 1945 (but I have my doubts).

Speck was sentenced to death on June 5, 1967, exactly one year before the assassination of Senator Robert F. Kennedy at the Ambassador Hotel in Los Angeles by another fall guy, Sirhan B. Sirhan. RFK died later that night, on June 6, 1968, or 6-6-68. Speck's execution was to take place 88 days later, on September 1, 1967, but his sentence was later commuted to 400 to 1200 years – a span separated by 800 years, another 8.

The hidden hand waves mockingly at us from behind a veil of symbolic numbers, dates, and saints. But once we learn to identify and interpret the signs, the laugh is on them.

CHAPTER EIGHT

STRANGE HISTORY

(Sections of this chapter are repeated from my book *Richard Speck and the Eight Nurses: Deconstructing A Mass Murder*).

The mass murder of the eight nurses was given the title of "crime of the century" by the coroner, and it stuck. But while one hundred years is a long time, memories are short. This title has been given to numerous crimes in the Twentieth Century.

And it's an interesting label. Like "Man of the Week," "Person of the Year," or "Most Valuable Player," our media loves to confer great honor to a heinous crime instead of judging it for the horror that it is. In July 1966 the terrible massacre of eight lovely young women received this dubious title as if it were some kind of twisted achievement. The development of this trope intrigued me, so I took a few trips down a rabbit hole to dig further into what other "crimes of the century" were really about. My findings suggest that catastrophic crimes, as tragic and horrible as they are, serve as tools for propagandizing various agendas, and they also share bizarre and intriguing connections.

What makes a good candidate for the designation of crime of the century? It has nothing to do with the enormity of the crime or the number of victims. Instead, certain crimes are nominated to promote sinister yet timely themes, insinuating that we are not safe around certain types of people (hippies, racial groups, the mentally ill, men, and so on). In this case eight young career-minded women were murdered in their dormitory, causing countless women to fear being alone, going out, even turning out the bedroom light. Countless others may have reconsidered becoming independent wage earners because it no longer felt safe for women to venture forth on their own.

To add insult to this injury, many people victim-blamed the nurses, all of whom were young, single, and pretty: They must have been having a wild party, they must have flirted with the wrong guy, they must have asked for it. Young women either risked being murdered, or risked the heavy-handed judgment of those who disapproved of women who were trying to advance themselves. The burgeoning feminist movement, which encouraged women to enter the male-dominated world of careers and business, received a direct shot across the bow, courtesy of the murders.

Crimes of the century also share a flair for the dramatic, as we have seen time and again in the present case – "All my friends are dead!" "It's the crime of the century!" "It's the greatest single sex crime in history!" and "This is the man!"

May 1889 – The Murder of Dr. P.H. Cronin

Dr. Patrick Henry Cronin emigrated from Ireland to Chicago, bringing his strong political leanings with him. He was a member of the clandestine societies of Clan na Gael and the Royal Arcanum and Chosen Friends, groups who supported the liberation of Ireland from British rule.

Cronin was murdered by political enemies, and became an Irish-American hero and martyr for his cause. His murder was highly publicized abroad, and many thousands attended his funeral, thus earning the title of "crime of the century." Ironically Cronin was a physician at Cook County Hospital in Chicago. Chicago was the birthplace of the first "crime of the century," and deservedly so. There would be more.

May 1924 – The Murder of Bobby Franks by Nathan Leopold and Richard Loeb

The setting for this vicious murder of fourteen-year-old Bobby Franks was again Chicago. Franks was the son of a wealthy neighbor of Nathan Leopold, 19, and Richard Loeb, 18, also of respectable, well-heeled families. Both young men were highly intelligent. Leopold had already graduated from the University of Chicago and Loeb, from the University of Michigan. But they were bored and disaffected with their lives, and began to commit petty crimes to see what they could get away with.

Gradually the risk-taking escalated to murder, and on May 21, 1924, they lured young Bobby Franks to a park where they strangled him and left his body in a culvert. A pair of eyeglasses found near the crime scene connected them to the killing, and they were convicted and sentenced to life in prison.

The notorious pair introduced the concept of the motiveless "thrill kill" murder to American society, and broke the stereotype of the common murderer as a low class, poorly educated, socially disadvantaged individual. It was widely rumored that Leopold and Loeb were homosexual lovers, a serious taboo in the 1920s that introduced another shocking element to the crime. Leopold and Loeb also considered themselves as intellectual supermen, an ideal lead-in to the fascist movement that was gathering traction at that time.

The idea that young, handsome, intelligent men of upper class breeding could callously murder a child no doubt set society on alert that killers could be anyone and lurk anywhere. Children were no longer safe at the hands of those who should have known better.

March 1932 – The Kidnap/Murder of Charles Lindbergh, Jr.

This crime occurred at the country home of famous aviator Charles Lindbergh in rural New Jersey. Lindbergh had gained enormous fame by being the first to cross the Atlantic Ocean non-stop in a solo flight; he was the rock star of his day.

On March 1, 1932 Charles Lindbergh, Jr., his two-and-a-half year-old firstborn son, was taken from his crib in a second floor bedroom and found dead in a wooded area some months later. German immigrant Bruno Richard Hauptmann was later convicted in a sensational "trial of the century" and executed in the electric chair.

Many investigations have since supported Hauptmann's innocence, implicating a high-level conspiracy and cover-up. They contend that Hauptmann was framed and that Charles Lindbergh Sr., whose sado-psychotic behavior has been revealed only in recent literature,had a hand in staging the crime. (p. 100 Pearlman) An avowed Nazi sympathizer, he was also a staunch supporter of the Nazi party and eugenics. In 1932, while Hitler was rising to power in Germany, German-Americans were viewed with suspicion. The German immigrant with the middle name of Richard had a criminal record in Germany, making him an ideal patsy.

And your child is not safe in his crib even if you're a national hero.

November 22, 1963 – Assassination of President John F. Kennedy

The numbers surface very quickly in this assassination, which took place on November 22, 1963, or 11-22. JFK was the 35th President – 3 + 5 = 8.

The assassination ultimately took place in Dallas, where Speck grew up, and was blamed entirely on Lee Harvey Oswald. The "lone gunman" trope was born of the JFK assassination, and passed on to Speck, then James Earl Ray and Sirhan B. Sirhan, to round out the assassinations and patsies of the Sixties.

DESPERATE RITES: ASTROLOGY AND THE OCCULT IN THE RICHARD SPECK MURDERS

JFK was supposed to be assassinated in Chicago first. Dallas, Speck's old haunting grounds, and New Orleans, both play prominent roles in this drama. Through his truck delivery job, Richard Speck knew Jack Ruby, who was originally from Chicago. The JFK assassination was likely motivated by a pro-war, right-wing faction, and Lee Harvey Oswald, a supposed Communist supporter, served as the patsy. The fear of Communism, firmly drilled into school children like myself during the 1950s, stoked the flames of war, and JFK's removal led to a hawkish President Johnson whose policies squeezed the lifeblood out of hundreds of thousands more victims of the Vietnam War.

August 8, 1969 – The Sharon Tate Murders

Needing a change of scenery, the crime of the century trope traveled west to Hollywood, land of illusion. Five individuals, including actress Sharon Tate, hairdresser Jay Sebring, coffee heiress Abigail Folger, friend Wojtech Frykowski, and Steven Parent, were brutally stabbed and shot at the home shared by Tate and her director husband, Roman Polanski, who was filming in London at the time.

Charles Manson and his ragged band of followers, known as the Family, were convicted of the murders. Although Manson was not present, he became the country's first mass murderer by proxy. Subsequent investigations have shown that the evidence was flimsy at best, and that the murders were possibly the result of a deeper, darker cult ritual. The only direct evidence was a confession by Family member Susan Atkins, a known grifter and liar. The murders had profound sociological impact, discrediting and bringing down the so-called "hippie movement" practically overnight, which was thought to be one of the prevailing motives behind the scenes.

Both crimes had powerful social ramifications that changed the thinking of American society; both involved sham trials with little concrete evidence but plenty of narrative shaped by powerful prosecutors and their media lackies. And both may have been influenced by right-wing supporters who wanted America to adopt a more hawkish attitude toward law, order, and war, thus bringing an end to the peace-loving, pacifist flower children.

The theme of passivity so strongly emphasized in the nurses' murders, a clumsy way to explain why eight women with everything to fight for chose not to fight, also shows another important feature of so-called crimes of the century - they do not support pacifism. They also introduce or feature some extreme ideology, like the fascist notions of a superior race, as shown in the Leopold/Loeb and Lindbergh cases, and the mass murder of the eight nurses.

The Manson narrative previewed a dystopian future that included a violent race war named after the Beatles' eponymous hit song "Helter Skelter". The Helter Skelter was actually a carnival ride, a spiral slide around a tower at a British amusement park. The song referenced confusion and disorientation, the type of feeling you might experience after careening down a spiral slide.

Manson's race war never took place, but the Manson affair inflicted damage on the American psyche, creating fear, panic, and the ever-increasing need for assurances of law and order, safety, and security in the face of a growing social chaos. All the crimes of the century served this purpose, greasing the slide of a communal helter skelter, leading us farther into a land of confusion, disorientation, and fear.

I suggest we beware when the moniker "crime of the century" is applied to a modern-day crime. So far, so-called crimes of the century have been tailor-made for high drama, and nothing invokes high drama like a fake narrative replete with misinformation and propaganda.

Sadly, what is real and true are the unfortunate victims. The rest is born of hyperbole, illusion and fakery spun by a dark cult. It's a magic show, where we sit mesmerized by what the magician's one hand is doing, totally oblivious to what the other, hidden hand is really up to.

What's In A Name

Here is where the correspondences between the crimes get even crazier. Besides the frequency of "crimes of the century" that took place in Chicago, and the recurring frequency of dark cult ideologies, we have a tangled nest of repeating names.

The name of famous aviator Charles Lindbergh's father was Carl August Mansson. Mansson changed his name to Lindbergh after he emigrated to the United States from Sweden in the 1800's.

As noted, Richard Franklin Speck temporarily assumed his stepfather Lindbergh's name and went by the name Richard Franklin Lindbergh for several years. The first arrest warrant issued by the FBI was in fact for Richard Franklin Lindbergh.

Baby Lindbergh Jr.'s convicted kidnapper/murderer was German like Speck, with the middle name Richard, and he was a fall guy too. The super race enters here too, with Lindbergh Sr.'s devotion to Nazi ideologies.

Just a few years after the mass murder of the nurses came Charles Manson, also linking by the Manson name to the Lindbergh and Speck cases. These three crimes of the century are strangely intertwined by names, but the seeming coincidences don't stop there.

Speck's biological father was Benjamin Franklin Speck. To honor him Speck adopted Franklin as his middle name, and for some years he went by the name Richard Franklin Lindbergh. When he married in 1962 he changed his name to Richard Benjamin Speck. Benjamin Franklin was an important name in the Speck generations, and as strange history bears it out, Richard was also an important name to the famous American statesman Benjamin Franklin.

Franklin made his fortune as a printer in Philadelphia. One of his earliest publications was "Poor Richard's Almanac". Apparently he liked the name Richard; he also wrote under the pen name Richard Saunders, which was oddly the name of a metaphysician and astrologer from the 1600's (Franklin dabbled in astrology, so I don't know whether the adoption of this name was coincidence or deliberate). To honor Franklin the U.S. Navy commissioned a freighter called the "Bonhomme Richard."

More correspondences abound between the two men. Benjamin Franklin established the first school of nursing in the colonies, and he was an active member and founder of the Lodge of the Nine Sisters, which promoted the study of science and art consistent with Masonic teachings. On the murder night there were nine student nurses in a townhouse that served as a dormitory for a nursing school.

Remember Speck's childhood address, 908 W. Boston Street? Benjamin Franklin was born and raised in Boston until the age of 17, and this number pervades his life story, as we will note shortly. 9 + 0 + 8 = 17, and power number 17 reduces to power number 8.

Born to Raise Hellfire

Part of Speck's legacy was his infamous tattoo, "Born to Raise Hell," which was also the title of a best-selling book by his psychiatrist, Dr. Marvin Ziporyn. Ben Franklin was an active member of London's notorious Hellfire Club, a private club where all manner of drinking, cross-dressing, and debauchery routinely took place. Both Speck and Franklin apparently loved to raise hell in their own way.

DESPERATE RITES: ASTROLOGY AND THE OCCULT IN THE RICHARD SPECK MURDERS

Among his many contributions Ben Franklin invented bifocal glasses, or spectacles, commonly referred to as "specs".

Franklin Benjamin Richards is a Marvel comics fictional character, a young superhero who is one of the most powerful beings in the universe. There's something uncanny about the affinity these three names have for each other, plus, the prominent theme of a superhero makes for an interesting association.

To digress a bit, many events in Ben Franklin's life feature the number 17. He was born on January 17, 1706 and died on April 17, 1790, which was the 107th day of the year, or 107 = 17. He ran away from home at the age of 17. He was appointed a Grand Master Freemason in 1731 (17, 31 / 13) of the London Grand Lodge of Freemasonry, which was founded on Saint John's Day, June 24, 1717. He lived for exactly 1011 months and one day, or 1111, and reportedly died at 11:00 PM, which is also 2300 hours, or 23. One might say that the man truly lived - and died - by the code.

For all we know, Hans Adam Spach, Speck's first German ancestor to set foot in this country, crossed paths with Ben Franklin in colonial Philadelphia. Ben Franklin's mother was Abiah Folger, making him a cousin to wealthy coffee heiress Abigail Folger, victim of the infamous Manson murders.

Abigail was murdered just two days shy of her 26th birthday (an 8), August 11, which can be shown as 811 or 118. This time 8 and 11 did not equal "life" either. The date of the Manson Family mass murder was August 9, 1969, or 8/9, another supercharged combination.

CHAPTER NINE
STRANGER THINGS

(This chapter is partially reprinted from my book *Richard Speck and the Eight Nurses: Deconstructing A Mass Murder*).

My Long, Strange Trip

If anything sums up my experiences exploring the deeply entangled web of this crime, it is that iconic song by the Grateful Dead, "What A Long Strange Trip It's Been." Driven by curiosity, I had embarked on a simple quest to learn more about the eight nurses whose murders had upset me so badly as a young girl. Understatement of the decade: I got way more than I bargained for.

As overwhelming as the project felt at times, circumstances constantly guided me in the right direction. I would open a book or a file, and instantly find the data I was seeking. Names and places that I was researching would pop up in seemingly unrelated television programs or books. I experienced a synchronicity with certain events that Carl Jung himself would have envied. Having made some startling discoveries, I chose to write this book, but in an odd way it also chose me.

Strange confirmations of this came from unexpected sources. While drafting the section on the Lindbergh baby kidnapping, I noted that it was March 1, 2022, the 90th anniversary of that "crime of the century."

It was the Lindbergh case that had inspired me to write my first crime astrology book back in 2012, *Forensics by the Stars,* which included a chapter on the kidnapping. My research pointed strongly to the conclusion that Bruno Richard Hauptmann, the convicted kidnapper/

killer, was framed. Little did I know that I would come to the same conclusion about Richard Lindbergh/Speck, who had once headlined my adolescent "Most Hated" list.

I researched the musical "Carousel" and its iconic song "You'll Never Walk Alone" on January 3, 2021. The song was recorded in 1965 by British rock band Gerry and the Pacemakers, and was one of Gloria Davy's favorite songs that she listened to just before meeting her tragic demise. I later heard that Gerry Marsden, lead singer of Gerry and the Pacemakers, passed away the very day that I researched his iconic song and its connection to this story.

During the same week in July 2021 that I was researching her Planned Parenthood Foundation, I learned that the name of its founder, Margaret Sanger, was unceremoniously expunged from the signage at its headquarters due to her racist views.

Sergeant Richard J. Oliva, witness for the prosecution, was born on the day my parents got married, and other connections to him exist via certain personal numbers.

Assistant State's Attorney William J. Martin, lead prosecutor of the case and co-author of the book *The Crime of the Century: Richard Speck and the Murders That Shocked the Nation*, which I have criticized in my previous book, passed away in 2017. His funeral service was held at Salerno's Galewood Chapel in Chicago - no relation.

The Moraine-on-the-Lake resort where Corazon Amurao stayed was located in Highland Park, Illinois, the same name of my town. There is also a hospital named after St. Camillus in Batangas, Philippines, home province of Corazon Amurao.

Since childhood I've had a small pen knife that is almost identical to the knife dredged up from the Calumet River and thought to be Speck's murder weapon. Just as I was completing my previous book I discovered that one blade bears the inscription "Camillus" – an eerie homage to the patron saint of nurses and hospitals featured in the story.

But my favorite woo-woo moment occurred when a friend called the day that I verified that Gene and Martha Thornton's Chicago address was 3966 N. Avondale Avenue. My friend left a message with her phone number. Her extension was 3966.

This continued during the preparation of the present work. On the day that I was writing the section on the number 33 I received an email from a realtor regarding a new listing. The address was 33. Later that same day I checked the stats for an interview I had recently given. It had received 3,300 views – another 33.

Odds and Ends

Gloria's father, Charles E. "Chuck" Davy, was a member of the Odd Fellows, a secret society under the umbrella of Freemasonry, the oldest such group of its kind in the United States. As trustee of the West Pullman Odd Fellows, Davy held a respectable position within the group.

Charles Davy was not the only closed society member on the periphery of the crime – one that I could discern, as there were probably others that I couldn't. Sergeant Richard J. Oliva, who testified that Speck had confronted him at the Shipyard Inn on the night of the murders, was a member of the Loyal Order of Moose, headquartered in Mooseheart, Illinois.

Membership requirements at that time were to be male, Caucasian, and have a military background. Like the Freemasons, joining the group required an elaborate ritual initiation. The Order of Moose command enormous wealth and political power in Illinois, including the ownership of schools, hospitals, office buildings, and numerous businesses, including a crime scene cleaner (thanks go to The Occult Rejects Youtube channel for their informative podcast in this regard).

Sergeant Oliva piqued my interest only because he testified to seeing Speck brandish both a small folding knife and the large hunting knife at the Shipyard Inn. But Speck had sold the large hunting knife earlier that same day. Patrick Walsh, friend of Oliva and another witness from the Shipyard Inn, testified that Speck brandished a gun and one knife.

Apparently Oliva was coached to introduce the large Navy-issue knife. Even though it played no role in the murders, the large knife, the biggest piece of non-evidence in this case, sent another red flag waving in my viewfinder.

This fact may lead nowhere, but the dots form an interesting cluster. Before entering the military, Oliva worked for a time at Republic Steel, where Gloria Davy's father, Charles Davy, was a manager. They may, or may not, have known each other; hundreds of men worked at Republic Steel in those days. This is probably one of those rare times that I can use the word coincidence, but it's still an item of interest.

Other patterns of interest ran in the Speck family. Speck lost his father Frank at the age of six, when Frank was only 53 years old. The cause of death was a heart attack, which claimed Speck himself on the day before his fiftieth birthday. Frank Speck had also lost his father Nathaniel when he was only two years old. Richard lost a brother, Robert Coleman Speck, to an auto accident when Robert was only twenty-four; father Frank had also lost his brother Nathaniel at an early age. Going back even further, we note the untimely death of a great uncle, Joseph J. Speck, who lived only nineteen years, from 1843 until 1862.

DESPERATE RITES: ASTROLOGY AND THE OCCULT IN THE RICHARD SPECK MURDERS

Speck had a shotgun wedding with sixteen-year-old Shirley Malone, who had gotten pregnant soon after they met. The birth of Speck's oldest sister predated his parents' wedding by just a few months.

The early loss of a child appears as a consistent pattern during the course of several Speck generations. Repeating threads and patterns in this crime story unfurl across time like one unending tapestry. It is no wonder that Speck's first ancestor in the New World, Hans Adam Spach, was a weaver.

EPILOGUE

Give Me That Old Time Religion

The numbers and occult symbols that appear throughout this crime story implicate a clandestine dark cult that adheres to practices established by ancient religions. These religions, based on pagan beliefs, did not support Judeo-Christian values. They operated based on symbolic dates, such as those discussed in this work; they sprinkled coded numbers throughout their constructed narratives; they paid homage to religious figures in their activities, usually, martyrs and victims of sacrifice.

Who were they? Luciferians, Satanists, Illuminati, the Process Church, Freemasons, Jesuits, Nazis? These groups have played in the same sandbox for centuries, so the answer is anyone's guess. Rather than speculate as to which dark cult destroyed eight innocent young lives to protect a covert agenda, my purpose has been to show how occult symbols and references feature in catastrophic crimes. Knowing what to look for gives us an added understanding of what the hidden hand is up to. It is no longer enough for terror cells or dark cults to drop their covert clues into a story – people are waking up and catching on. This work is my contribution to the wake-up call.

The rabbit holes of major crimes run deep and dirty, criss-crossing each other in unexpected ways that seemingly have no connection, yet connect. In Book One of his *Sinister Forces* trilogy, author Peter Levenda writes of this phenomenon, "Events are related by invisible threads of connection that link them in ways too subtle to be measured by the normal cause and effect paradigm with which we are all familiar." (p. 260)

The once invisible and well-concealed threads of connection of many misdeeds of the past are now finally coming to light and in fact, unraveling before our very eyes. It is a light that can't be extinguished. Even the power numbers tell us so.

"For nothing is hidden that will not be revealed, nor anything secret, that will not be known and come to light." Luke 8:17 = 8 and 17, or 8 and 1 + 7 = 88.

More powerful words were never spoken.

REFERENCES

Biedermann, Hans. *Dictionary of Symbolism: Cultural Icons and the Meanings Behind Them.* Penguin Books, 1992.

Bills, Rex E. *The Rulership Book.* Macoy Publishing and Masonic Supply Co., Inc., 1971.

Charubel and Sepharial. *The Degrees of the Zodiac Symbolized.* Astrology Classics, 2004.

Cirlot, J.E. *A Dictionary of Symbols.* Barnes & Noble, Inc., 1971.

Ebertin-Hoffman, *Fixed Stars and Their Interpretation.* American Federation of Astrologers, 1971.

Evans, Valerie. *Forensic Astrology 101: Using Timestamps to Investigate Unsolved Mysteries* ebook.

Jones, Marie D., and Larry Flaxman. *11:11 The Time Prompt Phenomenon.* New Page Books, 2009.

Levenda, Peter. *Sinister Forces: A Grimoire of American Political Witchcraft: Book One: The Nine.* Independent Publishers Group, 2005.

Levenda, Peter. *Unholy Alliance: A History of Nazi Involvement with the Occult.* Continuum International Publishing Group, 2007.

Robson, Vivian. *The Fixed Stars and Constellations in Astrology.* Samuel Weiser Inc., 1969.

Stojanovic, Nikola. *The Degrees Theory: The Secrets of the Exact Astrology.* Nine Horses Journey, 2017.

Teal, Celeste. *Eclipses: Predicting World Events and Personal Transformation.* Llewellyn Publications, 2009.

The Occult Rejects Youtube channel.

Westcott, W. Wynn. *Numbers: Their Occult Power and Mystic Virtues.* Theosophical Publishing Society, 1911.

All horoscope charts were created using Regulus Platinum Professional 7 software.

Don't miss out!

Visit the website below and you can sign up to receive emails whenever B D SALERNO publishes a new book. There's no charge and no obligation.

https://books2read.com/r/B-A-WFDW-BZKOC

BOOKS 2 READ

Connecting independent readers to independent writers.

Did you love *Desperate Rites: Astrology and the Occult in the Richard Speck Murders*? Then you should read *Richard Speck and the Eight Nurses: Deconstructing A Mass Murder* by B D SALERNO!

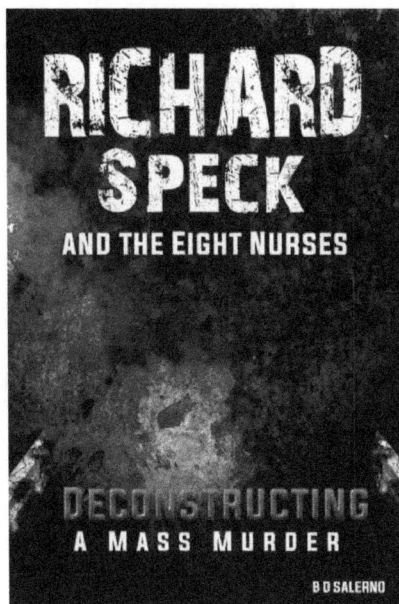

Late on the night of July 13, 1966, eight of nine student nurses were brutally murdered in their townhouse. They never screamed, they never fought, they never tried to run, and no one could understand why. The eight horrific murders were attributed to Richard Speck, a 24-year-old unemployed seaman with a long rap sheet. One nurse survived by hiding under a bed. She was the crux of the prosecution's case, a slam dunk that brought in a guilty verdict after only 47 minutes of jury deliberation.

In the decades that followed, no one studied all the inconsistencies between the police reports, the witness' testimony, the FBI files, the physical evidence, the autopsy findings, the newspaper articles, and the trial testimony. Not until now.

Author B.D. Salerno spent over three years studying sources and reference materials never before investigated, deconstructing the historical narrative that served as the official story of the crime. Her findings are nothing less than astounding.

If you are a true crime aficionado, you will appreciate reading about the author's discovery of the illicit activities that were taking place at the nurses' training hospital, and how these may have played a role in the mass murder.

You will learn how viable tips from influential authorities were ignored in an effort to pin the mass murder on one man, while the evidence screamed that several persons were involved. You will learn that certain evidence was questionable, while other viable evidence was ignored.

Eight promising young student nurses were brutally and senselessly murdered. But it didn't happen as we were told. Find out more about it here.

Also by B D SALERNO

Desperate Rites

Desperate Rites: Astrology and the Occult in the Richard Speck
Murders

Standalone

Richard Speck and the Eight Nurses: Deconstructing A Mass Murder
Richard Speck and the Eight Nurses: Deconstructing A Mass Murder
Anywhere But Here: Confessions of A Pisces Moon

About the Author

BD Salerno received her undergraduate and graduate education at Rutgers University and her secondary education in New York City, where she trained in medical massage therapy, acupuncture, and other holistic modalities. Her eclectic interests – alternative healing, astrology, and true crime - focus on understanding what makes things tick.

Salerno combined her love for astrology with her fascination for true crime and published two books on the astrology of crime: *Forensics by the Stars* in 2012 and *Exploring Forensic Astrology* in 2016.

In 2023, following three years of intensive research, she published *Richard Speck and the Eight Nurses: Deconstructing A Mass Murder*. The present work is a sequel that concentrates on the astrology of the crime and the occult symbols sprinkled throughout the crime narrative in the form of numbers, dates, religious references, and imagery.

www.ingramcontent.com/pod-product-compliance
Lightning Source LLC
Chambersburg PA
CBHW030024290326
41934CB00005B/469